T0299237

The Nature of Japanese Governance and Seikai-Tensin in Postwar Japan

What shapes characteristics and types of state governance in a specific country? How do they change over time? More importantly, what will they look like in the near and far future? This book addresses these fundamental yet timely questions by introducing and analyzing a distinctive group of Japanese statesmen: Seikai-Tensin, which means one's transformation into politicians in Japanese.

The book looks at the Japanese developmental state through a time-series analysis on historical data to determine the dynamic pattern of a prototype developmental state. It offers comparative implications for other developmental states, including South Korea and Singapore, to have a better understanding of themselves and their counterparts and useful lessons for governance practitioners to pursue a better balance between politics and administration.

This book will interest those researching governance, comparative politics, government bureaucracy, and public policy.

Nara Park is Assistant Professor of Public Policy and Management at Yonsei University, South Korea.

Routledge Focus on Public Governance in Asia
Series Editors:
Hong Liu, *Nanyang Technological University, Singapore*
Wenxuan Yu, *Xiamen University, China*

Focusing on new governance challenges, practices and experiences in and about a globalizing Asia, particularly East Asia and Southeast Asia, this focus series invites upcoming and established researchers all over the world to succinctly and comprehensively discuss important public administration and policy themes such as government administrative reform, public budgeting reform, government crisis management, public–private partnership, science and technology policy, technology-enabled public service delivery, public health and aging, talent management, and anti-corruption across Asian countries. The book series presents compact and concise content under 50,000 words long which has significant theoretical contributions to the governance theory with an Asian perspective and practical implications for administration and policy reform and innovation.

Sustainable Development Goal 3
Health and Well-being of Ageing in Hong Kong
Ben Y. F. Fong and Vincent T. S. Law

Mainland China's Taiwan Policy
From Peaceful Development to Selective Engagement
Xin Qiang

Public Administration and Governance in China
Chinese Insights with Global Perspectives
Leizhen Zang and Yanyan Gao

The Nature of Japanese Governance and Seikai-Tensin in Postwar Japan
Nara Park

For more information about this series, please visit www.routledge.com/Routledge-Focus-on-Public-Governance-in-Asia/book-series/RFPGA

The Nature of Japanese Governance and Seikai-Tensin in Postwar Japan

Nara Park

Routledge
Taylor & Francis Group

LONDON AND NEW YORK

First published 2023
by Routledge
4 Park Square, Milton Park, Abingdon, Oxon OX14 4RN

and by Routledge
605 Third Avenue, New York, NY 10158

Routledge is an imprint of the Taylor & Francis Group, an informa business

British Library Cataloguing-in-Publication Data
A catalogue record for this book is available from the British Library

ISBN: 978-1-032-33340-3 (hbk)
ISBN: 978-1-032-33341-0 (pbk)
ISBN: 978-1-003-31920-7 (ebk)

DOI: 10.4324/9781003319207

Typeset in Times New Roman
by Apex CoVantage, LLC

To Professor John F. Padgett

Contents

Figures

Tables

The author developed this book from her doctoral dissertation entitled "The Nature of Japanese Governance: Seikai-Tensin (政界転身)'s Political Success in Postwar Japan, 1947–2014" at the University of Chicago. The dissertation received the 2019 Carl Albert Dissertation Award from the Legislative Studies Section of the American Political Science Association.

1 Seikai-Tensin

From Bureaucrats to Politicians

Introduction

In shaping the nature of a civilized community, elite groups play a fundamental role. Historically, the majority of the records describe the operation of the state at that time, focusing primarily on the laws and systems enacted by the king and his officials. As modern state structures, especially democratic civil societies, were developed, the influence of non-elite groups became apparent. Elite groups, however, still play an important role in state politics, administration, and justice and determine the country's foreign and domestic policies. Therefore, it is essential to understand the nature of state governance of a country by understanding the characteristics of its elites.

Although Japan has produced many examples of grassroots democracy in recent decades, this elite-centered explanation may be more valid in many respects. As a modern country, Japan has been able to break out of its premodern past without undergoing bloody revolutions among the general population. This was during the Meiji Restoration (1868), a revolution by the emerging ruling elite group, which initiated the state modernization project in the mid-19th century. During this time, the foundations of a democratic state based on a constitutional monarchy were laid. The emerging ruling elite consisted of a subordinate responsible for overseeing the bureaucratic practices of the ruling samurai class at the time and emerged as the ruling elite after successfully replacing the previous ruling class, the senior samurai class. Among them, representative figures consolidated their governance bases by serving concurrently in major posts of the early modern Japanese government. Under the parliamentary cabinet system, where there is relatively little distance between the legislature and administrative functions, a phenomenon has been observed in which a small number of elites transcend the boundaries between political and administrative functions. Therefore, the political-administrative elites were not strictly distinct but rather converged within their own circles.

DOI: 10.4324/9781003319207-1

In this case, furthermore, meritocracy prevailed rather than the premodern practice of directly inheriting positions among these political-administrative elites. While the former aristocracy was granted a honorary rank (i.e., Kazoku, 華族) or a formal position (i.e., Kizokuin, 貴族院, the House of Peers), the new political-administrative elites were in charge of national decision-making. National educational institutions, most importantly the Imperial Universities, were established primarily to train elite officials during the early modern period in Japan. The elite officials gained recognition from the general public based on their practical competence. In spite of facing an existential crisis due to imperialism's rise and collapse, many of them eventually managed to remain on the administrative front, if not to enter politics, resulting in the amalgamation of politics and administration in the postwar period.

Overview of Seikai-Tensin

Political Success of Seikai-Tensin

Seikai-Tensin (政界転身) is an institutionalized phenomenon that illustrates the convergence of the Japanese political administration discussed previously. In its literal sense, Seikai-Tensin means a change of one's status in order to join politics, conventionally when the individual was previously employed as a bureaucrat. Essentially, it is the process of an administrative elite becoming a political elite. In fact, it is relatively common in Japan that retired officials often pursue a political career after retirement. Often, the phenomenon of Amakudari (天下り) is mentioned in relation to retired bureaucrats taking up good positions in the private sector after retirement, but it is distinguished from Seikai-Tensin, who move into politics after retirement.

Figure 1.1 displays that a considerable part of the National Diet of Japan has been filled in with Seikai-Tensin; approximately 20.2% of councillors and 16.9% of representatives are former government officials. Figure 1.2 shows that a group of new Seikai-Tensin has entered at a relatively constant rate at each election; about 19.1% for the Upper House and 14.1% for the Lower House were Seikai-Tensin among those who got elected to the Diet for the first time.

Attributes of Seikai-Tensin

Four Types of Seikai-Tensin Politicians

Table 1.1 summarizes the internal variations among Seikai-Tensin and illustrates examples of Seikai-Tensin's career paths. Although most Seikai-Tensin politicians follow a rather standardized career path, there are internal variations according to kinds and order of occupations that they assumed prior to the first election to the Diet.

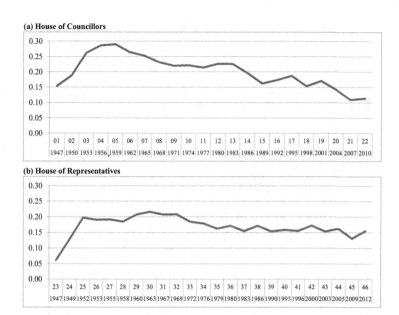

Figure 1.1 Proportion of Seikai-Tensin in the Japanese Diet

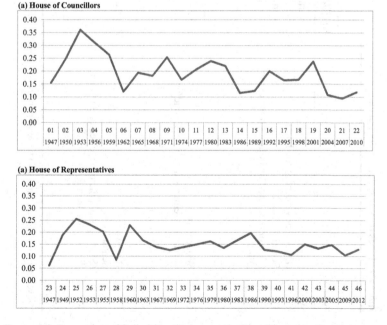

Figure 1.2 Proportion of Seikai-Tensin Among the First Elected to the Diet

Table 1.1 Types of Seikai-Tensin Politicians

Type	Career Path Before Election to the Diet			HC (%)	HR (%)
	First Job	→	Last Job		
A	Seikai-Tensin I (Direct movement to the Diet)	Government Official → →	Government Official	907 (78.6%)	1,417 (71.1%)
B	Seikai-Tensin II (One or more political offices prior to the Diet)	Government Official →	Elected Official - Legislator in the other house of the Diet - Local assemblyman - Politician - Mayor	131 (11.4%)	312 (15.7%)
C	Wataridori (Serial retirements in the public and/or private sector prior to the Diet)	Government Official →	Private Sector - Private company - Lawyer - Academia - Others	100 (8.7%)	165 (8.3%)
D	Backward Seikai-Tensin (Starting from the private sector and then direct movement to the Diet)	Private Sector →	Government Official	16 (1.4%)	99 (5.0%)
	Sum			1,154 (100%)	1,993 (100%)

*Government officials are limited to those working in the central government (ministry level).

A: SEIKAI-TENSIN I: DIRECT MOVEMENT TO THE DIET

Type A Seikai-Tensin politicians serve as central government officials for their entire career before becoming candidates for the Diet. It is the most typical form of Seikai-Tensin. To avoid confusion, Seikai-Tensin in this book refers to legislators who were previously career bureaucrats at the central government who afterward passed the Type I Civil Service Examination (国家公務員I種試験).[1]

B: SEIKAI-TENSIN II: A FEW MORE POLITICAL OFFICES BEFORE MOVING TO THE DIET

Type B Seikai-Tensin politicians are similar to Type A, except that they have run for elections for the other house of the Diet (either the Upper or Lower House), regional assemblies, governorship, mayorship, and so on. Therefore, in a strict sense, only Type A and B could be called Seikai-Tensin among the four types. In addition, as Table 1.1 shows, Seikai-Tensin politicians begin their career in the central government, and about half of them remain in the bureaucracy right before they are elected. Considering some Seikai-Tensin in the other half choose to be professional politicians mainly because they want to become members of the Diet, most Seikai-Tensin politicians commit themselves first to the government and then to the political world after their retirement.

C: WATARIDORI (渡り鳥): SERIAL RETIREMENTS IN THE PUBLIC AND/OR PRIVATE SECTOR

Type C Seikai-Tensin politicians go through a series of retirement steps in the public and/or private sector, as wataridori (i.e., migratory birds) travel across regions.

D: BACKWARD SEIKAI-TENSIN

Type D Seikai-Tensin politicians experience the inverse career path of Seikai-Tensin. While Type A and B Seikai-Tensin politicians move from the government to the political arena, Type D politicians move backward, from the political world to the bureaucracy. "Backward Seikai-Tensin" is not common, but it is interesting to note that there are those who take a reverse career path.

Comparison With Similar Cases: Quasi-Seikai-Tensin and Seshū-Giin

There are some similar cases to Seikai-Tensin, such as Quasi-Seikai-Tensin and seshū-giin. Table 1.1 does not include judges and prosecutors as Seikai-Tensin or Quasi-Seikai-Tensin, only cases where judges and prosecutors have worked at the ministry level, like the Ministry of Law (法務省) or Cabinet Legislative Bureau (内閣法制局). Nonetheless, we can expand the scope of Seikai-Tensin to include

Table 1.2 Seikai-Tensin vs. Non–Seikai-Tensin/Quasi–Seikai-Tensin

Type of Legislators	Seikai-Tensin	Quasi-Seikai-Tensin	Non–Seikai-Tensin
Number of Cases	• HC: 1,154 • HR: 1,993	• HC: 181 • HR: 427	• HC: 4,375 • HR: 9,381
Educational Background	*Tōdai* • HC: 67.85% • HR: 74.66% *Top 8** • HC: 87.00% • HR: 92.32% ≠	*Tōdai* • HC: 28.18% • HR: 16.63% *Top 8** • HC: 41.99% • HR: 59.95%	*Tōdai* • HC: 9.18% • HR: 10.62% *Top 8** • HC: 38.12% • HR: 60.42%
Party Affiliation	*LDP* • HC: 66.55% • HR: 61.97% ≠	*LDP* • HC: 30.94% • HR: 38.17%	*LDP* • HC: 34.00% • HR: 37.80%
Bureaucratic Background	Career Track ≠	Non–Career Track	None

* Top 8: The University of Tokyo (a.k.a. Tōdai), Kyoto University, Hitotsubashi University, Waseda University, Keio University, Chuo University, Meiji University, Nihon University.

bureaucrats like those who previously worked at the central government, but on contract terms (嘱託), and label them "Quasi-Seikai-Tensin" to show that working experience in the government per se does not qualify as a Seikai-Tensin. What matters is whether they are on the "career track". Table 1.2 shows that Seikai-Tensin politicians are significantly different from other members of the Diet in terms of their educational, political, and bureaucratic backgrounds.

A growing number of Japanese politicians are classified as hereditary politicians (seshū giin [世襲議員] or second-generation legislators, nisei giin [二世議員]). They inherit local political machines (kōenkai, 後援会) from their fathers or relatives who previously held congressional office in the district. For example, some former prime ministers, including Koizumi Junichirō and Abe Shinzō, are seshū giin from influential political families. As Table 1.3 displays, hereditary connections are not so relevant with Seikai-Tensin. Both of these groups of politicians make up a majority of elected legislators (in the Lower House) but rarely overlap with each other.

Historical Resilience of Seikai-Tensin

Seikai-Tensin is not an entirely postwar phenomenon. Seikai-Tensin's predominance dates from the very start of modern Japan. Table 1.4 shows that ex-bureaucrats occupied seats in the House from the Meiji period (1868–1912), and this continued to the Imperial period (1912–1934). Overall, the average proportion of Seikai-Tensin in the prewar House was about 10.9%.[2] This is

Table 1.3 Backgrounds of Japanese Representatives: Seikai-Tensin vs. Seshū-Giin

	1953	1967	1972	1983	1993	2000	2003
(a) Seikai-Tensin	60 (13.9%)	63 (13.0%)	59 (12.0%)	55 (10.8%)	79 (15.5%)	76 (15.8%)	70 (14.6%)
(b) Seshū-Giin	22 (5.1%)	61 (12.6%)	77 (15.7%)	119 (23.4%)	123 (24.1%)	117 (24.4%)	136 (28.3%)
(a) *AND* (b)	20 (4.6%)	13 (2.6%)	15 (3.1%)	11 (2.1%)	13 (2.6%)	16 (3.3%)	13 (2.71%)
(a) OR (b)	62 (14.4%)	111 (23.0%)	121 (24.6%)	163 (32.1%)	189 (37.0%)	177 (36.9%)	193 (40.2%)
Tōdai Graduates	100 (23.2%)	114 (23.6%)	108 (22.0%)	97 (19.1%)	94 (18.4%)	100 (20.8%)	93 (19.4%)
Total # of Reps	431 (100%)	483 (100%)	491 (100%)	508 (100%)	511 (100%)	480 (100%)	480 (100%)

Source: Modified from Usui and Colignon (2004); their analysis only includes ex-bureaucrats who are members of the Lower House of the LDP.

Table 1.4 Seikai-Tensin in the Prewar House, 1890–1946

Election No.	Election Year	HR Total	# of Seikai-Tensin	% of Seikai-Tensin
1	1890	300	48	15.9
2	1892	166	29	17.6
3	1894	265	33	12.3
4	1894		32	12.2
5	1898	258	23	9
6	1898		17	6.7
7	1902	228	19	8.5
8	1903	93	7	7.6
9	1904	120	10	8.4
10	1908	206	19	9.2
11	1912	196	21	10.9
12	1915	153	17	11.4
13	1917	151	15	10.2
14	1920	277	29	10.5
15	1924	252	37	14.6
16	1928	173	28	15.9
17	1930	127	18	14.1
18	1932	128	22	17.4
19	1936	127	18	13.9
20	1937	93	15	15.6
21	1942	202	31	15.3
22	1946	386	33	8.5
Average		195.0	23.7	10.9

Source: Ramsdell (1992).

approximately 6% point lower than that of the postwar House (16.9%). Still, it is interesting that Seikai-Tensin made an appearance starting from the pre-war period and survived until today. Given other types of government retirees, like Amakudari, were not institutionalized until the end of WWII (Inoki 1995), the early appearance and durability of Seikai-Tensin appear peculiar. What could explain this historical resilience of Seikai-Tensin's existence in modern Japan, including both prewar and postwar?

Considering that Seikai-Tensin began to appear from early modern Japan, it is highly likely it was caused by a historical and/or cultural legacy in the Tokugawa period (1603–1867) that preceded modern Japan. There are three factors that appear profoundly relevant to the development of Seikai-Tensin: 1) centralization, 2) bureaucratization, and 3) the blurring of politics and bureaucracy. The Tokugawa regime developed a vastly *centralized* structure within its feudal system. To manage the centralized feudalism for more than 250 years of Pax Tokugawa, the governance system was *bureaucratized*, and the samurai turned into bureaucrats. With centralized and bureaucratized arrangements, both top–down and bottom–up decision-making were institutionalized into the system. A top–down process tends to strengthen the power of political leadership, while bottom–up decision-making is led by the rank-and-file bureaucrats. Going back and forth between top-down and bottom-up, politicians and bureaucrats co-opt each other on various policy issues.

The three aspects continued unabated, going through rises and falls of the modern history of Japan. After the *Meiji Revolution* (1868), the founding fathers of modern Japan, who were born out of the lower samurai family, established centralized bureaucracy, from central to local, as a bedrock for their power and authority. As the Meiji oligarchy swept everywhere, the boundary of politics and bureaucracy became even more blurred. Decades later, the purge on war criminals and contributors during the *American occupation* (1945–1952) hardly affected the Japanese bureaucracy and its centralized governance system but was actually fortified, while the purge severely crushed the military and political circles. As a result of the heightened central bureaucracy, a hybrid of bureaucracy and politics emerged; this could be understood as a consequence of the "politicization of bureaucracy" and/or "bureaucratization of politics". There have been debates over whether and/or when *the 1955 system* collapsed (Kenji 2014). The Liberal Democratic Party (LDP) constituted the government and legislated jointly with central bureaucracy since 1955. The collapse of the 1955 system implies the weakening of central bureaucracy, which has been a main participant in the policy-making process partnered with the LDP. The LDP lost the government in 1993 and 2009 but each time returned not long after, and centralized bureaucracy within the government remained steadfast. Politics and bureaucracy work in concert with each other, and Seikai-Tensin still stood enduringly as a hybrid between the two realms. All considered, there has been consistency in centralization, bureaucratization, and the blurring of politics and bureaucracy since the Tokugawa period, and this has not dwindled through a transition from premodern to modern, from prewar to postwar, and from LDP rule to multiple-party rule in Japan.

Roadmap of the Book

In Chapter 2, the origins of Seikai-Tensin politicians are traced all the way back to the prewar period, the Meiji era, and even the Tokugawa period. There are deep roots in Japan's history as a country of samurai, and Seikai-Tensin is part of that culture, which respects bureaucrats. 1) Centralization, 2) bureaucratization, and 3) the blurring of politics and bureaucracy are chosen as primary sources for the Seikai-Tensin's continued prevalence in postwar Japan. These three factors have exhibited a striking consistency when viewed through the lens of historical institutionalism. There were critical junctures in Japanese history that could have disrupted the path dependency and shaken the foundations for Seikai-Tensin's existence; however, these critical junctures did not lead to a discontinuity in the factors discussed previously. As critical junctures of modern Japan, 1) the Meiji Revolution and the accompanying reforms (1868), 2) the American occupation and purging of war criminals (1945), and 3) the (temporary) collapse of the 1955 system (once in 1993 and then 2009) are discussed.

Chapter 3 deals with the first step in Seikai-Tensin's political career: his or her election to the Diet. Having bureaucratic and ministerial experience increases one's likelihood of election significantly. One's political affiliation, however, especially with the LDP, has the greatest influence on their election. Legislative activities do not have a significant influence on elections; activities outside the floor, such as committee work, may be helpful but are not of great significance. Although education generally does not matter for one's election, graduating from the University of Tokyo would be electorally advantageous if the person also has other elite attributes such as bureaucratic experience and/or membership in the LDP. Put simply, Seikai-Tensin's multiple elite qualities help them gain votes. Elections can result in a transformation from the bureaucratic elite to political elite. Therefore, elite qualities beget one another, reshaping the elite as a whole.

Chapter 4 focuses on the next phase (or the last except for the premiership): cabinet appointments and ministerial tenure. The purpose of this chapter is to examine the effects of bureaucratic background on 1) legislators' likelihood of receiving the first ministership and subsequent appointments and 2) their duration in the cabinet after they are appointed. Most importantly, bureaucratic background plays a significant role in cabinet appointments.

A Seikai-Tensin minister would not remain in a given cabinet for very long, however. Although there are other factors that affect individual ministers' duration, the "Seikai-Tensin effect" would hold strong in cabinet appointments and tenure in the long run. In general, Seikai-Tensin held more ministerial posts than non–Seikai-Tensin; and their ministerial tenures in cabinet were on average longer than non–Seikai-Tensin's.

Chapter 5 explores Seikai-Tensin's motivation and decision to shape their career paths and social institutions. Their decision makes sense both from a personal interest and for the (pragmatic) public good. They choose a bureaucratic profession because it can satisfy both their personal interests and their desire to contribute to society. There could be a number of reasons they leave the government, such as frustration with the bureaucracy, a desire to reform politics, and concerns about their careers. This provides a different perspective on Japanese governance than developmental state theory (DST). It is argued by DST that the dramatic economic growth of some East Asian countries in the late 20th century was fueled by bureaucratic autonomy. The existence of Seikai-Tensin, however, indicates the complementarity of politics and administration, which describes a foundation of the Japanese governance at both the macro level (social institutions) and micro level (personal motivations).

Notes

1 There are three types of examination to become a bureaucrat in Japan: Type I (for four-year college graduates), Type II (for two-year college graduates), and Type III (for high school graduates). "In contemporary Japan, all government officials must pass entrance examinations, but the old system is perpetuated by a differentiation between the difficulty and comprehensiveness of the examination taken ... those who pass the first (type of examination) and are accepted by a ministry may advance to the highest executive levels of the career service, including the position of vice-minister, but those who pass the second (and the third type of examination) cannot be promoted beyond the section chief level, and usually not that high" (Johnson 1982, 58).
2 The House of Peers, the counterpart of the House of Councillors of today, is not covered in this study. It drew its members from the Imperial Family, the Peers, people who paid high taxes, and others appointed by the emperor. The prewar Lower House had less strict restrictions on background its members. The former had people with nobility and loyalty, while the latter had room for people with merits, such as bureaucrats.

Works Cited

Inoki, Takenori (1995). "Japanese Bureaucrats at Retirement: The Mobility of Human Resources from Central Government to Public Corporations," In *The Civil Service and Economic Development: Catalysts of Change*. (1st ed.). Hyung-Ki Kim, Michio Muramatsu, T. J. Pempel, and Kozo Yamamura (eds.). (Oxford: Clarendon Press).

Kenji, Gotō 後藤謙次 (2014). *The Collapsing 55 System* 『崩壊する 55 年体制』. (Tokyo: Iwanami Shōten 岩波書店) (Written in Japanese).

Ramsdell, Daniel B. (1992). *The Japanese Diet: Stability and Change in the Japanese House of Representative, 1890–1990.* (Lanham: University Press of America).

Usui, C., and R. A. Colignon (2004). "Continuity and Change in Paths to High Political Office: Ex-Bureaucrats and Hereditary Politicians in Japan," *Asian Business & Management,* 3(4): 395–416.

2 Emergence and Evolution of Seikai-Tensin

Introduction

This chapter investigates the changes and continuity of Seikai-Tensin in the history of Japan. In Chapter 1, we saw three defining features of Japanese politics and bureaucracy with regard to the nature of the ruling class, governance system, and national decision-making process. Chapter 2 will show how those defining aspects have been institutionally reinforced in modern times. A lack of dramatic changes, however, is not the cause of the institutional reinforcement and the resulting institutional consistency. Indeed, Japan has gone through a lot of dramatic changes since 1868, like any other country around the world. Despite the critical junctures, however, Japanese modern political history has displayed continuity rather than change, which led to an institutional reinforcement of centralization and bureaucratization stemming from the premodern legacies.

As such, over the course of their continued existence, Seikai-Tensin have been related to other political *actors* as well as the existing *institutional set-up*. Also, the way these actors relate to other actors and affiliated institutions would have affected the institutions' relationship *vis-à-vis* other institutions. Having a *dual identity*, Seikai-Tensin, as ex-bureaucrat politicians, would have played a certain role in relation to networks of actors and institutions of politics and bureaucracy.

Demystifying Well-Founded Myths About the Premodern Japanese State: Centralization and Bureaucratization

This section will debunk three well-founded myths about the premodern Japanese state, starting from the Tokugawa period. The reason to choose the Tokugawa period as a starting point is largely twofold. First, during this period, Japan oversaw the longest peace and stability in its history, which is likely the most influential on the modern and contemporary Japanese state.

DOI: 10.4324/9781003319207-2

Second, the Tokugawa would arguably be the most well-known historical era but is also one of the most misunderstood periods; many would likely have an image of the belligerent samurai to represent the whole Tokugawa period or the whole premodern Japan.

There are three myths to be unmasked in this section. First, the samurai were not only warriors but also bureaucrats, as opposed to the common knowledge that premodern Japan was a country of samurai. Differently put, the premodern Japanese ruling class—encompassing kuge (the court nobles) and buke (the military nobles)—was not entirely militaristic but also bureaucratic. Second, a popular misconception, that premodern Japan was a *typical* feudal society, will be addressed by arguing that Japanese feudalism differed from its counterpart in medieval Europe in that it had a much more centralized system of government with a legitimate authority. Third, for students of Japanese politics and the government, it is a misunderstanding to view Japanese decision-making as a bottom–up process because it is essentially *top-down*, with critical decisions made at the top, while necessary tasks are divided across different levels of decision-making.

Demystification I: Nature of the Ruling Class—The Samurai as Both Warriors and Bureaucrats

This section will introduce a historical fact that the samurai should be regarded both as warriors *and* bureaucrats. As a primary reason, one can suggest the long-lasting peace sustained in the Tokugawa period without imminent threats of internal and external military conflicts. As a clear piece of evidence that warriors do not entirely occupy the ruling class in the premodern times, this section will shed light on the upper-level samurai, kuge, who are distinguished from buke.

Pax Tokugawa: Prolonged Peace and the Fate of the Warriors

As stated previously, the Tokugawa bakufu was the longest-lasting regime in Japanese premodern history. After the victory by Tokugawa Ieyasu (徳川家康) in the Battle of Sekigahara (関ヶ原の戦い) in 1600, Japan was finally unified. The Tokugawa unification finalized the era of Sengoku (1467–1603), literally meaning a warring state, which was symbolized by incessant military mutinies for well over 100 years. Fearing any further military conflicts against himself, Tokugawa Ieyasu made every effort to establish strong centralization within his regime to put local powers, that is, any potential military threats, under his control, employing various means, which will be discussed at length in the next section. This attempt, as proven by history, was successful. As a result, the Tokugawa period, named after the Tokugawa shogunate, lasted for more than 250 years.

The prolonged peace maintained by a strong state brought about an unintended consequence: *a country without a war does not need a warrior*. During the period, Japan had no war inside or outside (Brown 1988).[1] Due to idleness, a *refunctionality*[2] for the samurai had to be found, since they were too strong to be removed but too impractical to maintain as they had been. The samurai had to be transformed, at least partially, *from warriors to bureaucrats* to perform a governing role in the new, peaceful regime. "The number of offices steadily increased, in part to provide employment for the samurai. The shogunal administration alone eventually comprised some 17,000 positions" (Fulcher 1988, 231). All in all, bureaucratization was essential in the Tokugawa regime, which was a highly stable and centralized state. *State formation begat elite transformation* (Higley and Burton 2006, 20).

There is a term that shows the elite transformation in the Tokugawa regime was quite peculiar compared to other neighboring countries. In the Sinosphere, the term Shinōkōshō (士農工商) indicates four occupations in premodern society, in the order of strict social strata: *shi* (士) for scholars, *nō* (農) for farmers, *kō* (工) for artisans, and *shō* (商) for tradesmen. In China and other countries with the Confucian tradition, *shi* (士) refers to "a man of letters" (文士). They take the highest place in the social strata since only scholars could apply for governmental offices, especially for high-profile ones. Bureaucrats were highly respected in the Sinosphere, as the term *kanson-minpi* (官尊民卑) denotes.[3] There were offices for "men of swords" (武士), but they were limited in terms of the number of posts and status within the government. This, however, was quite different in premodern Japan. As stated, the bakufu government was primarily staffed with the samurai, or men of swords (武士). So *shi* (士) indicates warriors (武士) rather than scholars (文士) in the Japanese context.[4] Some scholars (文士) were also recruited by the government but mostly as advisors or assistants to the samurai at the upper level.

Some *incorrectly* view that samurai only denotes the warrior class at low levels, which distinguishes them from other descendants of the warrior class such as shogun, daimyō, and buke. This view, however, should be modified, as the aforementioned three labels are actually used to denote different levels in the samurai classification. Essentially, shogun and daimyō are also samurai. As such, Tokugawa Ieyasu himself and recognized founding contributors—who were either shogun, daimyō, or buke—can all be classified as samurai, with some distinctive internal differentiation. Simply put, samurai refers to lower-rank warriors, but it can also be used to indicate the overall warrior class, with internal stratifications. The samurai at the top played a more political role than an administrative one, which was assumed by the lower-class samurai. The line between politics and administration was blurred in the premodern Japanese government.

As a precaution, there are two things to note. First, although they worked as bureaucrats, a militaristic feature is an integral part of the samurai's identity, more than anything else. Put differently, the source of their identity comes from being soldiers, while their being bureaucrats is a function that they perform. Second, we can find a bureaucratic tradition from the samurai, but in many ways, they are different from the ideal type of Weberian bureaucrat in modern times.[5] The samurai worked for their shogun or daimyō,[6] and their fidelity was rather personal, whereas modern bureaucracy does not and should not feature loyalty to an individual. The samurai were recruited primarily because of their birth, and remuneration and promotion were given to their status as samurai rather than their office.[7] In contrast, most modern bureaucracies, in their ideal forms, are supposed to operate based on meritocracy.

Dual Nobility: Kuge and Buke

The samurai[8] would be the first thing that comes to one's mind if one tried to imagine *traditional* Japan. Japan has largely been described as a country of the samurai, who reigned for thousands of years, starting long before the Tokugawa period began. The samurai rule in the premodern era is a defining feature characterizing every aspect of Japan, from history to culture, society, and politics, and from ancient times to the contemporary period. The samurai, indeed, have repeatedly been depicted as heroic characters in legendary tales, involving a rather mythic image in countless books and movies reproduced in and outside of Japan.

Nonetheless, the samurai, arguably being a dominant class for the most of premodern Japan, have never been the sole ruling class in Japanese history. This is not a newly discovered fact, as it was already uncovered by previous research and has been established in the literature. Nonetheless, one important implication of this fact is there was, at the very least, another lineage of nobility that could be seen as parallel to—though it cannot be equated with—the samurai as the warrior class: kuge (公家).

Kuge, as opposed to buke (武家), referring to the high nobility in the militaristic heritage, were also premodern aristocrats in Japan. Kuge were nobles affiliated with the Imperial court located in Kyōto, whereas buke were warrior nobles who resided either in the bakufu government in Edo or the han governments in local provinces. Simply put, kuge is largely distinguished from buke (i.e., the most prestigious warrior families) or the samurai in a more general sense. Tokugawa Japan, from 1603 to 1867, can be depicted as *diarchy* of kuge and buke rather than *pure monarchy* by the shogun. In fact, this "dual-authority system (the shogunal-military and imperial-civil) . . . had existed since 1192 when Minamoto Yoritomo established the military government, or bakufu (shogunate), in Kamakura" (Lebra 1993, 28; capitalization added by the author), and it was firmly institutionalized in the Tokugawa period.

As a matter of fact, kuge and buke significantly differ from each other. To begin with, aside from hereditary factors, kuge and buke had a seemingly very different source of power and legitimacy thereof; kuge relied on their literary knowledge with a humanistic worldview, whereas buke primarily possessed a power based on their martial skills and achievements during wartime; in particular, military merits gained during the battle of Sekigahara (関ヶ原の戦い, 1600) were a decisive factor in ranking the samurai. Second, although they were both public officials in governmental institutions, and kuge and buke were both the highest nobility from each clan, they differed in terms of their magnitude in the government and the level of offices they could assume within the governmental hierarchy. Said another way, the samurai, or a more general term for buke, were prevalent in the premodern Japanese government, while kuge did not have a lower counterpart to the samurai.

To summarize, one should not be misled by the predominance of the samurai but should note two important facts about them. First, the samurai, including buke, did not make up the whole ruling class in premodern Japan. There was kuge, another race of nobility different from buke. Second, but not less important, the Japanese ruling class in premodern times—including kuge, buke, and the samurai in general—essentially were all bureaucrats at various levels. *The prolonged peace transformed warriors into bureaucrats.* In a word, being premodern nobility in Japan was something more than just being brutally combative and aggressive. The samurai were not only warriors but also bureaucrats.

Demystification II: Nature of the Governance System—Centralized Feudalism

Japan developed a feudal system, which was more or less similar to the European one. The shogun, the one and only head of the bakufu government, whose succession is wholly decided by hereditary factors, is often equated with a king of European feudalism, while the daimyō, the head of each han government, can be equated with European lords or nobles. The samurai, with their own code of conduct called bushidō (武士道), are considered knights with chivalry. The shogun ruled the country in a rather decentralized and indirect way by allowing the daimyō to have their own lands and people. Given these points, one could say that it seems to be perfectly equivalent to European feudalism. Upon closer inspection, however, one would find that European feudalism and Japanese feudalism vastly differ; Japanese feudalism features a quite *centralized* form of governance. This section will investigate three centralization measures established in the Tokugawa feudal system with regard to their control mechanism of regions, nobles, and estates.

Domain Classification: Shinpan, Fudai, and Tozama

There are many more centralized elements in Japanese feudalism than in its counterparts in medieval Europe. First of all, from its outset, the Japanese feudal system was carefully designed with a consideration of strong shogunal control over each domain. When the Tokugawa regime was first established, daimyō of local parcels were classified into three strata—shinpan (親藩), fudai (譜代), and tozama (外様)—according to the degree of their presumed allegiance to the shogun. The first criterion for the classification was birth; shinpan daimyō were related to the Tokugawa family by blood, whereas fudai and tozama were not. There was a reason that made shinpan daimyō dependable to the Tokugawa; they were collateral relatives to the Tokugawa, so they were assumed to be set aside from the line to the throne. Put simply, shinpan were close enough to the ruling family but not so much as to be threatening to the shogunal power.

The second criterion for the classification was devotion displayed in the Battle of Sekigahara (関ヶ原の戦い) in 1600. In the battle, fudai daimyō fought *with* Tokugawa Ieyasu, either as his vassals or allies, while tozama daimyō did not. Tozama did not necessarily fight *against* the Tokugawa, but a membership in the Tokugawa alliance in 1600 drew a clear line between their own fates and fudai's for the next centuries. For example, unlike fudai, tozama daimyō were not allowed to hold office in the bakufu government. In short, with the deliberate categorization discriminating against local lords, the bakufu government in the capital city could effectively control them in a very centralized way. Notably, the shogunate placed fudai daimyō at strategic locations for geopolitical reasons, while tozama were relatively free from the central government's dispositional tactics.

In the end, however, the destiny of tozama was not severely ill fated, as expected at the beginning of the Tokugawa regime. That is because the bakufu government strove to pull together so that its regime could be maintained peacefully, and we know its efforts paid off. For a start, initial sanctions against tozama domains became relaxed over time, as the Tokugawa shogunate succeeded in building a cooperative relationship with them through carrots(i.e., marriages and guaranteed local autonomy) and sticks (i.e., control mechanisms such as sankin-kōtai [参勤交代], which will be explained in the next section). Next, although there was a clear division between fudai and tozama, especially in terms of governmental positions that they could assume, this does not imply that tozama were worse off than fudai, or vice versa. As the political status of daimyō did not entirely match up with the size of the fief and production thereof, *some* tozama daimyō possessed more lands and wealth than fudai daimyō.

Daimyō in Edo: Sankin-Kōtai (参勤交代)

Gradual homogenization across the local domains, either fudai or tozama, was in fact quite willfully managed by the central government. As such, most, if not all, state-building apparatuses of the Tokugawa regime were built to create centralized feudalism. Among others, sankin-kōtai was one of the most systematic forces that drove all the domains and their lords under central control by the bakufu. Sankin-kōtai made it compulsory for daimyō and their family members to inhabit Edo. Daimyō were allowed to return to their fief every alternate year, as the term sankin-kōtai's literal meaning, alternate attendances, denotes. Still, their families were required to remain in Edo for all time. This is one of the most distinctive features of Japanese feudalism that marks a difference from its European counterpart.[9]

By holding daimyō and their family members hostage in Edo, the bakufu was able to keep daimyō, or potential rebellions, at arm's length. Most importantly, however, the bakufu was able to effectively deprive daimyō of resources to wage war against them. First, the statute specified a certain living standard for daimyō residing in Edo (i.e., the size of their houses, number of retainers, kind of textiles that they could use for their clothes, etc.), which was set as quite sumptuous.

Second, their annual processions from and to Edo were very costly. Table 2.1 shows that local daimyō made a costly trip every other year to fulfill their sankin-kōtai obligation. It could differ depending on distance from Edo, but on average, processions (two-way) cost 5%–20% of the domain revenue. It goes up even higher to 50%–75% of revenues when costs of living in Edo are included. Additionally, daimyō were compelled to bring their samurai in accordance with their possessions, measured by agricultural production of their domains. The number of people included in processions ranged from a few hundreds to thousands. Given that processions took up to a month, it was quite burdensome for many domains, if not all, to fund travel from and to Edo. Taken together, sankin-kōtai was intended to incapacitate local powers and thus prevent any possible violent uprisings; history proved that this was surprisingly successful.

Table 2.1 Costs of Sankin-Kōtai

Domain	Distance From Edo (one-way)	Days of Travel to Edo (one-way, average)	Size of Processions (No. of people)
Sendai (伊達家・仙台藩)	368 km (92 里)	8–9 days	2,000–3,000
Kanazawa (前田家・加賀藩)	480 km (119 villages)	13 days	2,000–4,000
Tottori (池田家・鳥取藩)	720 km (180 villages)	22 days	700
Uwajima (伊達家・宇和島藩)	1,020 km (255 里)	30 days	300–500
Kagoshima (島津家・薩摩藩)	1,700 km (440 里)	40–60 days	1,800–1900

Source: Uwajima City History and Culture Lecture Series (2011).

Compensation for Loyalty: Rice, Not Land

A central feature in Japanese feudalism is also observable in the way that compensation was made for vassals' loyalty. Koku (石) is a Japanese unit of rice that is considered comparable to an amount that an adult consumes per annum; technically it is 150 kilograms or 278.3 liters. Koku was also used to measure potential production of domains, assessed by the quality and size of lands, and the system called kokudaka (石高) was a system developed for stipend distribution and taxation, using koku as a parameter. In brief, koku is a unit of rice, and kokudaka is government machinery operating based upon koku, not the land that produces rice.[10] Kokudaka was applied not only to local domains (thus to their lord daimyō) but also to individual vassals working at han governments in the local. The size of koku was the criteria differentiating samurai classes. Samurai households were also classified by the size of koku; for instance, they were called a 50-koku family, 100-koku family, and so forth. In other words, "distinctions in social status were reflected in income, with 100–125 koku representing the dividing point" (Silberman 1964, 15) between the upper and lower samurai. In particular, 80%–90% of the samurai were below 100 koku, and they performed highly administrative functions (吏務) such as security guards, procurement, and bookkeeping (Watanabe 2010).

An important implication from the kokudaka system is that the Tokugawa state provided their vassals, at different levels, with a limited form of remuneration. Koku is neither *ownership* of land nor a *right* to exploit the revenue that the land produces, but it is an *actual* commodity (i.e., rice or its equivalent) from the land. The first two forms of rewards may be equated with the third in terms of their monetary value, but they are to give more autonomy to their subordinates by allowing them to have a more capacity to utilize the given resources. In other words, the first two allow more leverage than the last one because they can be used for more various purposes, including a military purpose. Hence, the shogunate, at the core of centralized feudalism, clearly did not prefer those two forms of remuneration to the kokudaka system.

Demystification III: Nature of the National Decision-Making—Top-Down vs. Bottom-Up

In the previous sections, we have seen that Japan is a quite centralized (in terms of its *governance structure*) and bureaucratized (in terms of its *ruling class*) country, and we can find the root of those two traditions from the Tokugawa period, at the latest. Thus we now know who the decision-makers were and how their decisions have been implemented since the Tokugawa period. This section will uncover a misconception about the Japanese decision-making *process*, which has been assumed to be bottom-up, and argue that it is in fact a combination of top-down and bottom-up. As discussed in the following, there is room for the Japanese decision-making process to be interpreted either as top-down or bottom-up, especially because it actually fluctuates between the two extremes.

Struggle for Power: Top-Down vs. Bottom-Up

Organizational decision-making process and the outcomes thereof essentially reflect power dynamics within the focal organization. Depending on the given power structure, the decision-making process could be democratic or autocratic, horizontal or vertical, top-down or bottom-up, or some mixture of all these dimensions. Differently put, it is classified according to the locus of actual power on decision-making, where a real decision-maker is located.

In that regard, it would be interesting to look at the decision-making process in Japanese politics and government to understand the power relationship among actors within them (i.e., politicians and bureaucrats). Relatively speaking, in a top-down process: politicians predominate, while bureaucrats prevail in a bottom-up process. To be more specific, the former type of decision-making, where politicians are stronger, entails a process in which decisions are made first at the top and minutiae are filled in later at a lower level, whereas in the latter types of decision-making, details are determined earlier. Simply put, "top" or "bottom" denotes where the process starts.

Powerful Bureaucrats: Bottom-Up Decision-Making

Traditionally, Japanese decision-making has been described as bottom-up rather than top-down. One corollary of high-level centralization and bureaucratization is that there is a well-established chain of command by which decisions are funneled from top through the bottom; vertical stratification is regarded as essential to run a pyramidal organization efficiently. That is to say, top-down decision-making is conceived as being common in a typical bureaucratic organization. As such, many would take it as being odd that Japanese decision-making is considered bottom-up rather than top-down.

Ringi (稟議) is a particular style of Japanese decision-making as a bottom-up process. Originally it referred to a process in which a decision is made via a circulation of a document, ringi-sho (稟議書), among *all* members within an organization, usually from bottom to top. In particular, the ringi system seems to give more power to people at the bottom, as they initially draft the document. The document is circulated upward through a series of approvals, which is marked as a seal (hanko, 判子) of each person at various levels. When the document reaches the top of the organization, the decision is finalized, and all the members involved in the process are aware of that. The circular system seems to be highly democratic, as all individuals can participate in the process. In a certain sense, upper middle managers can be regarded as mere "rubber stampers" of the document drafted by the rank and file.

This system has deeper roots than one may think. Burton and Thakur (1998, 124–126) trace back to the Tokugawa period for a historical root for the ringi system. Heads of the autocratic bakufu government absolved themselves of responsibilities by entrusting administrative matters to their subordinates. If something went wrong, they could save face and thus retain their power by dismissing their subordinates who appeared to be most responsible for the task. This evasion tendency is not the case anymore in modern Japanese organizations, as supervisors are not free from joint liabilities, but the old customs to delegate decision-making to subordinates continue to today.

Additionally, ringi does not *exclusively* involve a vertical sequence of approvals. Ringi-sho, the document being circulated, is passed along to other sections or departments at equal levels. The intuition behind this *bi-directional* mechanism is that consensus building with all relevant actors involved is essential, which is largely consonant with the communal nature of Japanese culture. In sum, given the origin point (i.e., the bottom rather than the top) and the direction of the process (i.e., not only vertical but also horizontal), we can conclude that the ringi system, the traditional Japanese bottom-up decision-making procedure, is quite democratic by its very nature.

Powerful Politicians: Top-Down Decision-Making

If you take a closer look, however, the ringi system will reveal an utterly different aspect. That is, it can be interpreted as a top-down process. The aforementioned perspective points to the fact that an initiator of the decision-making process is the one who generates the first draft, which would remain unchanged until the final stage. In contrast, some would argue that you should look at what happens *before* the rank-and-file bureaucrat gets to start writing the first draft. According to them, a core idea for any important policy comes from the middle management, if not the top executive, and is delegated to his or her subordinates for further research and/or *mere* paperwork. While it is largely "synonymous with decision-making from below", "it appears to have been a process in which the major function of the superior official was to allocate problems to appropriate lower ranking specialists for solution" (Silberman 1973, 251). So from this perspective, the initiator of the whole decision-making process is the one who proposes a new idea first and is able to command others to do the rest of work.

The bakufu system revolved around a formidable political (or military) leader such as the shogun at the top and daimyō at the local level. The relationship between leaders and their followers (kashin: 家臣) was bounded with chivalry, called bushidō. The followers pledged absolute fidelity to their lord and were willing to die to show their allegiance if need be. In these master–servant relationships, commands from the lord have absolute authority, and kashin cannot help but follow orders. There were no political discussions inside or outside of the government, and at times only a few political powers had small meetings to make decisions (Park 2014).

In addition, informality precedes formality in Japan, both in terms of timing and importance. While the ringi system is a formal procedure involving a series of seals stamped on a document by all relevant individuals, there is an informal consensus-building process, nemawashi (根回し). Before initiating the formal authorization process, all responsible individuals mutually make a pre-arrangement on the idea proposed by the management or executive. More often than not, there is room for the rank and file to actively take part in the deliberation, but their chance of actual interference is limited in substance. In other words, the ringi system is just a matter of formality, whereas nemawashi substantively shapes real decision-making. On the surface, a drafter of an official document may look like a decision-maker. But in fact, a decision, made by senior members of organization in advance, is conveyed to the drafters, who merely translate the decision into a formal procedure, which requires tedious paperwork. Through delegation, the rank-and-file drafters may have a seemingly huge amount of leverage in writing an initial document, but the extent of their autonomy is significantly constrained by a boundary previously set by nemawashi. Simply put, drafters at a low level have a discretionary capacity as far as their superiors would allow; thus there essentially exists a certain limitation to their power regarding the decision being made.

Critical Junctures in Japanese Modern History and Institutional Reinforcement of Centralization and Bureaucratization

According to historical institutionalism, a change is usually initiated during critical junctures, which are "relatively short periods of time during which there is a substantially heightened probability that agents' choices will affect the outcomes of interest" (Capoccia and Kelemen 2007, 348). Once the direction for changes has been established, there is a high probability that institutional patterns will be set on a certain path and reproduced over time through self-reinforcing sequences (Mahoney 2000, 511).

It has not been uncommon to use the conceptual framework of historical institutionalism to examine the evolution of the Japanese political system. For example, Krauss and Pekkanen (2011) prove that the shift in the functions of candidate-support organizations, factions, and decision-making bodies of the LDP was a result of path-dependent processes that lasted for decades. Woodall (2014, 22–23) distinguishes eight historical junctures that were vital for changes in Japan's cabinet system, two of which—the Meiji Restoration in 1868 and American occupation in 1945–1952—had the characteristics of abrupt exogenous shocks. Schoppa (2011, 14–42), in turn, explains how path dependence prevented the formation of a party system based on clear cleavages on economic policy in post–Cold War Japan. While there is no consensus among scholars regarding what kinds of events are salient enough to initiate an institutional change, landslide electoral victories that provide mandates for policy alteration are usually considered critical junctures (Donnelly and Hogan 2012, 328; Cortell and Peterson 1999, 184).

This will tackle with three critical moments in modern Japanese history, which could have led to sweeping structural changes but ended up only with modest effects. The critical junctures have affected Japanese politics and the government, but this section will evaluate them in terms of the changes *vis-à-vis* centralization and bureaucratization, both of whose roots can be found in premodern Japanese history. In short, continuity prevails over discontinuity, as long as it comes to the Japanese tradition of centralization and bureaucratization.

Institutional Reinforcement I: Meiji Institutionalization of Centralization and Bureaucratization

As the previous demystification revealed, the Japanese state has *tradition-ally* been bureaucratic and centralized, perhaps much more so than one may think. This section will delve deeper into the long-standing tradition of centralization and bureaucratization of Japan by looking at the period following the Tokugawa period (i.e., the Meiji period) and by parsing how the heritage of centralization and bureaucratization has been institutionalized within the modern Japanese political system, on which this book primarily draws. In spite of so much volatility involved in modern Japanese history, one would find more continuity than discontinuity in the way that statesmen at the outset of modern Japan strove to design their own country.

More Than a Revolution: Meiji Restoration and Reformation

No one would deny that the year 1868 marks *the* starting point of modern Japan. Interpretation of what happened in 1868, however, is different according to how one intends to interpret the meaning of the beginning of Japanese modernity. Some would prefer to term it the Meiji *Revolution* to emphasize the upheaval in 1868 and the revolutionary social mobility displayed by the lower samurai from *the ragged to golden*. Others would prefer the Meiji *Restoration* over other terms in that it stresses the emperor as the spiritual pillar of the newly created Japan. The term Meiji *Reformation* underscores reformatory attempts and outcomes thereof during the period.

REVOLUTION

The term Meiji[11] Revolution signifies the *revolutionary* changes brought about by the lower samurai, who led an upheaval to overthrow the bakufu government. Their uprisings put a clear end to the Tokugawa rule, which lasted more than 250 years by force, and created irreversible transformations to Japanese history. Especially, it's worth noting that the majority of the *revolutionaries* were from lower ranks of the premodern status order. The changes in the composition of the elite would not have been possible without the Revolution.

Tables 2.2 through 2.4 show that five tozama hans (the most affected areas of Tokugawa discrimination policy) predominate offices in the early Meiji governments between 1868 and 1871, both at the higher and lower level. Simply put, the lower samurai, who were mostly career bureaucrats in tozama hans, including Chōshū and Satsuma, succeeded in military mutinies, and they thrived in Japanese politics from that time onward. In this regard, the Revolution was a milestone not only of modern Japan but also of bureaucrats' continued yet elevated rule in the modern era. The Meiji oligarchy "was homogeneous in age, social origin and political experience. The fact was vital to the success of the new government, for it gave a consistency and continuity to its actions which enabled fresh habits to become deep-rooted" (Beasley 1963, 105).

Table 2.2 Hometowns of Bureaucrats in the Early Meiji Governments, 1868–1871

	San Shoku	Shichi Ka	Hachi Kyoku	Dajōkan	Ni Kan Roku Shō	Sum (Mean)
Satsuma	10 (7.41%)	8 (13.11%)	11 (11.58%)	15 (7.89%)	26 (14.29%)	70 (10.86%)
Chōshū	6 (4.44%)	6 (9.84%)	5 (5.26%)	8 (4.21%)	18 (9.89%)	43 (6.73%)
Hizen	5 (3.70%)	0 (0.00%)	6 (6.32%)	14 (7.37%)	18 (9.89%)	43 (5.46%)
Tosa	4 (2.96%)	4 (6.56%)	4 (4.21%)	14 (7.37%)	11 (6.04%)	37 (5.43%)
Echizen	7 (5.19%)	4 (6.56%)	5 (5.26%)	6 (3.16%)	4 (2.20%)	26 (4.47%)
Sum	135	61	95	190	182	663

Note: This table displays only the five tozama hans. See Wilson (1957) for fuller information.

Table 2.3 Top Six Hans High-Tier Officials Came From

	San Shoku	Shichi Ka	Hachi Kyoku	Dajōkan	Ni Kan Roku Shō	Sum (%)
Aki	68	1	0	3	2	74 (16.67)
Hizen	7	0	0	13	16	36 (8.10)
Satsuma	0	1	0	12	20	33 (7.43)
Chōshū	4	0	0	8	18	30 (6.76)
Tosa	0	1	0	11	10	22 (4.95)
Echizen	7	1	0	5	3	16 (3.60)
Sum	135	26	13	130	140	444 (100.00)

Note: This table displays only the top six hans high-tier officials came from. See Wilson (1957) for fuller information.

Table 2.4 Top Six Hans Low-Tier Officials Came From

	San Shoku	Shichi Ka	Hachi Kyoku	Dajōkan	Ni Kan Roku Shō	Sum (%)
Satsuma	0	7	11	3	6	27 (12.33)
Kumamoto	0	3	7	0	2	12 (5.48)
Chōshū	0	6	5	0	0	11 (5.02)
Tosa	0	3	4	3	1	11 (5.02)
Echizen	0	3	5	1	1	10 (4.57)
Hizen	0	0	6	1	2	9 (4.11)
Sum	0	35	82	60	42	219 (100.00)

Note: This table displays only the top six hans low-tier officials came from. See Wilson (1957) for fuller information.

Nonetheless, another huge change was made to the composition of the elite in early modern Japan in terms of personal background. In his statements about the Japanese government between 1873 and 1894, Beasley (1963) found that

> it does not appear that the men of Satsuma and Chōshū [pronunciation mark added] had any overwhelming advantage, except at the very top. For the majority, the determining factors were ability, experience and loyalty, not geography or inherited status.
>
> (127)

Silberman (1964)[12] clarifies factors affecting the elite mobility of this period were non-traditional skills and knowledge such as "[l]earning of Western languages, technical skills and administrative skills; [p]articipation in activities and/or offices which were non-traditional in character". In order to qualify for the upper-level positions in the civil service that were created with the advent of the new government, Japanese would have to acquire skills and educational qualifications that were not readily available through the traditional institutional framework (Silberman 1964).

In summary, the lower samurai from tozama han with new knowledge and skills were the founding fathers of modern Japan. At the very core of Revolution, there was a combination of a successful coup through belligerent acts and foresighted preparation though non-traditional education. The Meiji leadership, most of whom were from the lower samurai, themselves acquired these non-traditional skills and education, and those became compulsory requirements for bureaucrats that they recruited for their government. Once again, *state formation begat elite transformation*. Continued from the Tokugawa period, bureaucrats played a key role in the Meiji regime, but the new era required new qualifications for bureaucrats. As the government was filled with those of ability, however, Meiji Japan began to turn into Japan as we know it today.

RESTORATION

The Meiji Revolution has another name: the Meiji Restoration. While the Revolution emphasizes dramatic and rapid changes caused by the revolt of the lower samurai, Restoration speaks to the *core* spirit of the movement. Under the slogan of Sonnō-Jōi (尊王攘夷, Revere the Emperor Dispel the Outsiders from the West), the revolutionaries, mostly the lower ranks of samurai, attacked the shogun in Edo to replace him with the emperor in Kyōto. Because of their humble origins, the revolting samurai were in need of political legitimacy in taking over the government; the Meiji emperor was enthroned in the year of 1868 and became their source of authentic power afterward.

It seems to be a great coincidence that a new emperor was inaugurated in the year of the Revolution and thus of a new era. As a matter of fact, Emperor Kōmei (孝明), the father and predecessor of Emperor Meiji (明治), met with an untimely demise. It is widely believed that Emperor Kōmei did not die of natural causes, as he was in excellent health even right before his death, and he was only 36 years old. It is believed that he was poisoned by the Meiji rebels, who desired to establish a solid foundation of their political power by helping a young prince ascend to the throne so that they could effectively put him under their control. Emperor Kōmei's sudden death left a vacancy, which was filled by his son, Prince Sachinomiya (祐宮), later designated Meiji. Emperor Meiji was 14 years old at the time of enthronement. The young emperor was the chief of state on paper, but actual decision-making was in the hands of the powers that be, as the Meiji revolutionaries allegedly intended. Simply put, it was "Personal Rule by the Emperor" (Tennō Shinsai, 天皇親裁; capitalization and Chinese character added by the author), which in practice meant that all decisions were made by a handful of leaders in the Council of State (Craig 1986, 50), or the Meiji oligarchy.

In brief, the allegations imply that the Meiji insurgents created a symbol of revolution by themselves by having Meiji as their emperor. It may sound ironic that modernizers wished to restore monarchy in establishing a new country. That obviously goes counter to *modern* state-building in the West. Restoration of the imperial power becomes even more ironic considering the fact that the modernizers were eager to imitate the modernization path of Western countries, which was primarily triggered by a collapse of absolute monarchy.[13] Said another way, the Japanese founding fathers created a *premodern* symbol to establish a *modern* country, that is, Emperor Meiji. The symbol was reinforced when titles of reformative policies, institutions, and laws (e.g., the Meiji Constitution, the Meiji Shrine, etc.) were named after Emperor Meiji. That is because political reformers had to seek justification for their actions in the ancient history of Japan, and the emperor was the best figure that symbolized the *legitimate* tradition.[14]

REFORMATION

The Meiji Ishin (明治維新), meaning reformation in Japanese, is arguably the official term referring to the 1868 outbreak. Ishin literally means a major overhaul and has the most similar meaning to Reformation among the previously mentioned terms. This points to the fact that the founding fathers intended "drastic changes" to lie at the heart of the newly constructed modern Japan. Notwithstanding, changes brought about by the Reformation display a double-sided ambiguity; it was meant to be modernization in a highly Westernized way, but it also demonstrates a *retro* style in many aspects.

First and foremost, Japanese modernization can be equated with Westernization, which led to numerous adoptions of Western institutions, including the modern bureaucracy and parliament. As a result of their modernization efforts, by the end of the Meiji period, "there were few organizations in the major Western industrial societies that did not have their counterparts in Japan" (Westney 1987, 5).

Still, the imitation was not entirely servile, in that reproduction went through a very selective process based both on rationality and patriotism. As William Foote Whyte succinctly puts, "Japanese change agents carefully examined models from more advanced countries, and selected some in terms of their judgment of what would best fit into Japan" (cited in Westney 1987, 5). That is, their rational consideration was combined with historical legacies tracing back to the past when the emperor had real power. "The new leaders, initially uncertain as to just what form of government should be built, first revived the emperor-centered features of the ancient Nara court with its system of daijokan (the state council), then later decided to assimilate the Western model." (Lebra 1993, 29).[15]

The Samurai as Founding Fathers: Centralization and Bureaucratization at the Top

The titular head of state was the emperor, but substantive power resided in the samurai who had revolted, who served as imperial advisors. Additionally, in 1873, Emperor Meiji moved from the Kyōto palace to the Akasaka palace in Tōkyō and never returned (or was never able to return), which was in fact the Meiji revolutionaries' decision. This implies that the imperial power was captured by the revolutionaries. The emperor's residency in Tōkyō made it easier for them to seize power, as all the central authorities (i.e., the emperor and themselves) were gathered around the capital city, whereas the Tokugawa had the diarchy of the shogunate in Tōkyō vs. the emperor in Kyōto, with the clear predominance of the former. In short, the emperor's moving from Kyōto to Tōkyō finalized the centralization of governmental entities. The centralization was planned and achieved by those who had been the lower samurai in premodern times.[16]

The central government in Tōkyō grew bigger than the Tokugawa bakufu government in terms of its size and functions. Accordingly, the internal structure became bureaucratized to meet need for enlargement. The Meiji government started recruiting career bureaucrats based on meritocratic criteria in 1887. There was no limitation to qualifications of applicants, but many of them were descendants of the samurai because they were better suited for public office than any other classes at the outset of modern Japan, because "urban life, educational opportunity, and high achievement expectations combined to make it so" (Craig 1986, 90). Because "one had to be able to afford six years of schooling—three of higher, or preparatory, school and three of university work", most students at Tōdai were in fact "the sons of upper and upper-middle-class families" (Inoki 1964, 295–296). Takane (1976)[17] claims that ascriptive factors of feudal status influenced political status as late as 1936.

The Sat-Chō oligarchy, or the Meiji revolutionaries from Satsuma and Chōshū han, formed an informal body of genrō (元老, elder statesmen). The official purpose of genrō was publicized as offering advice to the emperor, but in effect, they were known to be a group of actual decision-makers of the Meiji government. Phrases such as "the power behind the throne", commanders of the inner circle", or "the real rulers of Japan" are used to describe genrō (Hacket 1998, 4). There were

> seven original Genrō (by order of birth): Matsukata Masayoshi (松方正義, 1835–1924), Inoue Kaoru (井上馨, 1836–1915), Yamagata Aritomo (山縣有朋, 1838–1922), Kuroda Kiyotaka (黒田清隆, 1840–1900), Itō Hirobumi (伊藤博文, 1841–1909), Ōyama Iwao (大山巌, 1842–1916), and Saigō Tsugumichi (西郷従道, 1843–1902). Later additions to the list always include Saionji Kimmochi (西郷従道, 1849–1940) and, more often than not, Katsura Tarō (桂太郎, 1848–1913).
>
> (Hacket 1998, 5; Chinese characters added by the author)[18]

Table 2.5 shows that the so-called Sat-Chō oligarchy was made up of genrō, and humble backgrounds predominated. In formal political

Table 2.5 Political Leadership in Genrō, 1889–1940

Name	Background	Hometown	Tenure in Genrō*
Itō Hirobumi	Lowest Samurai	Chōshū	1889–1909
Kuroda Kiyotaka	Lower Samurai	Satsuma	1889–1900
Yamagata Aritomo	Lowest Samurai	Chōshū	1891–1922
Saigo Tsugumichi	Lower Samurai	Satsuma	1892–1902
Matsutaka Masayoshi	Lower Samurai	Satsuma	1898–1924
Inoue Kaoru	Middling Samurai	Chōshū	1904–1915
Ōyama Iwao	Lower Samurai	Satsuma	1912–1916
Katsura Taro	Middling Samurai	Chōshū	1912–1912
Saionji Kimmochi	Top Aristocrat (Kazoku 清華家)	Kyōto	1912–1940

*In order of their first year in genrō.

Table 2.6 Meiji Premiership, 1871–1898

Name	Background	Hometown	Tenure in Genrō
Sanjō Sanetomi	Top Aristocrat (Kazoku 清華家)	Kyōto	07/29/1871–12/22/1885
Itō Hirobumi	Lowest Samurai	Chōshū	12/22/1885–04/30/1888
Kuroda Kiyotaka	Lower Samurai	Satsuma	04/30/1888–10/25/1889
Yamagata Aritomo	Lowest Samurai	Chōshū	12/24/1889–05/06/1891
Matsutaka Masayoshi	Lower Samurai	Satsuma	05/06/1891–08/08/1892
Itō Hirobumi	Lowest Samurai	Chōshū	08/08/1892–08/31/1896
Matsutaka Masayoshi	Lower Samurai	Satsuma	09/18/1896–01/12/1896
Itō Hirobumi	Lowest Samurai	Chōshū	01/12/1898–06/31/1898

Source: Modified from Woodall (2014, 51).

institutions such as the premiership, members of genrō were also dominant, as Table 2.6 displays. "All of the original seven members between them, at one time or another prior to 1900, held all the major posts in the civil and military bureaucracy and the government" (Silberman 1967, 82), and "their influence extended beyond the central bureaucracy" (Hacket 1998, 7).

Although it certainly was a sweeping change that the samurai, as a lower-level warrior class, arose as a new public official candidate pool, Tables 2.5 and 2.6 show that the Japanese founding fathers made very deliberate efforts to maintain a balance at the top of the state apparatus while creating a new order within. Considering hometowns, there were several alternations between Satsuma and Chōshū groups, both in genrō appointments and premierships, though there was one exception either at the beginning or the end of the period. This pattern is not a result of coincidence but of a carefully calculated scheme.

Table 2.7 corroborates this claim. Using Wilson (1957)'s data, the table analyzes the biographical background of bureaucrats in the early Meiji governments from 1868–1871. The ex-samurai formed the greatest part, 44.72% of the early Meiji governmental personnel. Great transformation in the governing leadership was achieved, seemingly all at once, from the very beginning of the regime. Nonetheless, the cells below the samurai reveal another fact, which seems to be at odds with the aforementioned finding. That is, along with radical change, persistence is also found, which would ensure stability and/or consistency at the time of the revolution. Among others, the ex-kuge, or premodern senior officials at the Imperial court, seem to be predominant, perhaps because of both their expertise and nobility. In short, there are *not only changes but continuity* in the recruitment of the early Meiji governments.

Table 2.7 Bureaucrats in the Early Meiji Governments by Class, 1868–1871

	San Shoku	Shichi Ka	Hachi Kyoku	Dajōkan	Ni Kan Roku Shō	Mean
Samurai	49	29	46	65	104	293
	(36.30)	(47.54)	(48.42)	(34.21)	(57.14)	(44.72)
Court Nobles	61	16	29	72	49	227
	(45.19)	(26.23)	(30.53)	(37.89)	(26.92)	(33.35)
Daimyō	8	2	5	20	3	38
	(5.93)	(3.28)	(5.26)	(10.53)	(1.65)	(5.33)
Ex-Daimyō	5	3	4	13	8	33
	(3.70)	(4.92)	(4.21)	(6.84)	(4.40)	(4.81)
Designated Heirs to Daimyates	4	2	3	8	4	21
	(2.96)	(3.28)	(3.16)	(4.21)	(2.20)	(3.16)
Princes of the Blood	6	5	4	1	2	18
	(4.44)	(8.20)	(4.21)	(0.53	(1.10)	(3.70)
Former Bakufu Officials	0	0	0	6	6	12
	(0.00)	(0.00)	(0.00)	(3.16)	(3.30)	(1.29)
Shinto Priests	1	4	2	0	1	8
	(0.74)	(6.56)	(2.11)	(0.00)	(0.55)	(1.99)
Commoners	0	0	1	1	4	6
	(0.00)	(0.00)	(1.05)	(0.53)	(2.20)	(0.76)
Younger Brothers of Daimyō	1	0	1	2	0	4
	(0.74)	(0.00)	(1.05)	(1.05)	(0.00)	(0.57)
Confucian Scholars	0	0	0	2	1	3
	(0.00)	(0.00)	(0.00)	(1.05)	(0.55)	(0.32)
Sum	135	61	95	190	182	663
	(100.00)	(100.00)	(100.00)	(100.00)	(100.00)	(100.00)

Note: Written by the author based on Wilson (1957)'s list of early Meiji bureaucrats.

Table 2.8 Proportion of Bureaucrats in the Early Meiji Governments by Class and Tier of Office, 1868–1871

Class	Tier	San Shoku	Shichi Ka	Hachi Kyoku	Daijōkan	Ni Kan Roku Shō	Mean
Court Nobles	High	45.19	53.85	61.54	28.46	24.29	42.66
	Low	0.00	5.71	25.61	28.46	24.29	16.81
Samurai	High	36.30	0.00	0.00	44.62	61.43	28.47
	Low	0.00	82.86	56.10	44.62	61.43	49.00
Princes of the Blood	High	4.44	19.23	30.77	0.77	1.43	11.33
	Low	0.00	0.00	0.00	0.77	1.43	0.44
Ex-Daimyō	High	3.70	11.54	0.00	7.69	3.57	5.30
	Low	0.00	0.00	4.88	7.69	3.57	3.23
Daimyō	High	5.93	3.85	0.00	12.31	1.43	4.70
	Low	0.00	2.86	6.10	12.31	1.43	4.54
Designated Heirs to Daimyates	High	2.96	7.69	0.00	3.85	0.71	3.04
	Low	0.00	0.00	3.66	3.85	0.71	1.64
Shinto Priests	High	0.74	3.85	7.69	0.00	0.71	2.60
	Low	0.00	8.57	1.22	0.00	0.71	2.10
Former Bakufu Officials	High	0.00	0.00	0.00	0.00	3.57	0.71
	Low	0.00	0.00	0.00	0.00	3.57	0.71
Younger Brothers of Daimyō	High	0.74	0.00	0.00	1.54	0.00	0.46
	Low	0.00	0.00	1.22	1.54	0.00	0.55
Commoners	High	0.00	0.00	0.00	0.00	2.14	0.43
	Low	0.00	0.00	1.22	0.00	2.14	0.67
Confucian Scholars	High	0.00	0.00	0.00	0.77	0.71	0.30
	Low	0.00	0.00	0.00	0.77	0.71	0.30
Sum	High	100.00	100.00	100.00	100.00	100.00	100.00
	Low	100.00	100.00	100.00	100.00	100.00	100.00

Note: Written by the author based on Wilson (1957)'s list of early Meiji bureaucrats.

Table 2.8 shows that, despite the sweeping dominance of the ex-samurai in the overall government system, shown previously, further breakdown discloses a rather different pattern. On average, in the five early Meiji governments, the ex-kuge, or court nobles, top the chart (42.66%) in the high tier of the government system. This was affected by absence of ex-samurai in the two governments, 0% for Shichi Ka (七科) and Hachi Kyoku (八局) This pattern is reversed in the last two governments—Daijōkan (太政官, 44.62%) and Ni Kan Roku Shō (二官六省, 61.43%); the samurai vastly prevail. In the low tier, however, the ex-samurai always outnumbered the ex-kuge. Accordingly, ex-samurai occupied the most offices in the low level.

*In short, ex-samurai held a stable majority at the lower level, while the high
tier was vastly filled by ex-kuge.*

The End of Feudalism: Centralization and Bureaucratization of Local Administration

Centralized feudalism came to an end when the founding fathers established
the central government.

> The capitulation of the buke to the emerging regime was marked by
> three major events: the taisei hokan of 1867 (the "reverential" return of
> the shogunal government to the imperial court); the hanseki hokan of
> 1869 (the reverential return of domains to the court); and haihan chiken,
> in 1871, replacing the domains (han) by prefectures (ken).
>
> (Lebra 1993, 29)

Among the three, hanseki hōkan and haihan chiken affected daimyō in a
rather direct way.

The tozama hans, including Satsuma, Chōshū, Tosa, and Hizen, led the
way by voluntarily yielding their lands and people to the emperor. They
clarified that it is natural to return them to the emperor, who innately owns
the right to them by the law of God. In parallel with the implicit yet coer-
cive command, they persuaded the other hans through kōgisho (公議所), a
deliberation council. The Meiji government offered pecuniary compensa-
tions (i.e., rice and cash) *quid pro quo* in their cooperation in building the
new government. Officially, the compensation was provided as reparation
for their contribution (賞典禄) to the Boshin war (戊辰戦争); hence, the
hans were rewarded retroactively. Many historians, however, argue that the
nature of the rewards was rather proactive in order to ensure cooperation
for state-building in progress. The negotiations went quite well, and this
land reform, called hanseki hōkan (版籍奉還), was successfully completed.

With the lands returned to the emperor, or a *symbolic* icon of the Meiji
revolutionaries, the existing premodern administrative districts were gradually abolished. The title of this policy, haihan chiken (廃藩置県), literally
means that feudal domains (藩) were abolished and modern provinces (県)
established. In 1871, haihan chiken was accomplished at the national level,
and the Ministry of Home Affairs (Naimushō, 内務省) was established
in 1873 to govern the newly established administrative districts (Katsuta
2002).

After yielding their lands and people, many daimyō were transformed
from hereditary feudal lords to government-appointed governors of their
fiefs. It was one the strategies that the Meiji government utilized to maintain

stability by sustaining feudal elements to some extent. However, the governors were replaced by public officials from the Ministry of Home Affairs. Instead, daimyō were given an honorary title, kazoku (華族), and a set of privileges, including a right to enter the House of Peers (貴族院) with life tenure. Despite this, they were never able to regain their lands, people, or jurisdictions. At the end of WWII, the kazoku system and the House of Peers were abolished, and they even lost their status as an aristocratic class.

> Thus, by midsummer of 1871, the work of centralizing governmental authority in Japan was complete: a single monolithic bureaucracy stretched downward from a handful of decision-makers with authoritarian powers, through ministries headed by samurai ministers, to prefectures with appointed governors, and then to the districts and villages, or cities and wards.
>
> (Craig 1986, 58)

Summary and Implications

Taken together, it is true that medieval Japan prior to 1868 was a feudal society and that active centralization attempts were made only after the Meiji period. It was not an easy task to transform a premodern feudal society into modern state with centralized system, even if one could accept that Japanese feudalism had centralized elements and this may have helped the Meiji revolutionaries realize centralization. The data in this section show how the Meiji state was established and developed into a modern society. First, the political leadership of the Sat-Chō oligarchy was very cohesive, and their influence was far reaching. Centralized bureaucratic institutions made their reign easier, as they could assume posts as heads of a ministry to control them. Beginning with the central bureaucracy, they took the control of the entire administration from top to local. "The origins of this group in the bureaucracy and their continued influence over it made the dividing line between bureaucracy and government almost indistinguishable for the greater part of this period" (Silberman 1967, 82). "This blurring of the lines between bureaucracy and political leadership had in fact been a feature of the Tokugawa shogunate, though the actual composition of the group of high officials had obviously changed" (Fulcher 1988, 234). In a word, the Meiji regime had both changes and continuity from the Tokugawa period, in terms of *centralization, bureaucratization, and the blurred border of politics and bureaucracy.*

Second, the Meiji revolutionaries did not abandon feudal society at once but exerted many of efforts to incorporate feudal elements into their centralization policy. This again helped the Meiji revolutionaries to push forward balanced measures between feudal and modern and between decentralized and centralized. It was how they could be so successful in achieving desired centralization within only a few years, without great social friction among classes and regions. The Meiji government did not hesitate to make departures from premodern Japan but did not relentlessly rush either. From personnel to organization, their careful approach to achieving balanced development was one of the biggest factors of their success.

Institutional Reinforcement II: American Occupation and Postwar Continuity

The Japanese state went through dramatic changes at the outset of the modern era. The country was closed (sakoku: 鎖国) until the end of Tokugawa regime and then was widely opened, modernized, and westernized by the Meiji revolutionaries. The openness turned into an expansive strategy toward East Asia and the world without any intermediate stages. The modern government system established by the founding fathers was refined and settled through war preparation. The centralized bureaucratization, rooted in the premodern history of Japan, continued in the Imperial period.[19] This expansion plan, seemingly successful at a certain point, was brought to an end by the emperor's speech (Gyokuon Hōsō: 玉音放送) declaring an unconditional withdrawal from WWII. This section will move on to the year of 1945, in the aftermath of WWII and the following occupation by the General Headquarters (GHQ) of the Allied forces.

Purges After WWII

Sweeping changes were expected after Japan's surrender to the Allied powers. The Constitution of Japan was drafted by Americans[20] under the Occupation by the GHQ, which also compiled lists of Japanese war criminals of WWII. The lists were used to prosecute "Class A" war criminals and to purge collaborators in a broader sense. The number of purgees who were prohibited from assuming public office was over 20,000 between 1946 and 1952 (Dower and Hirata 2007). The range was quite broad to include those in the public and private sectors. Many leading political figures were purged and never returned.

Returns Soon After the Purge

Having that said, however, the effects of purge did not last long. The purge officially ended in 1952, and a number of purgees were exempted and returned. Eighty percent of the members of the House of Representatives were purged, but their families ran for election; thus their seats were only lost on paper.

As for the bureaucracy, the aftereffect of purge was even more restricted, for the following two reasons. First, the purge on bureaucrats was limited in the first place. Bureaucrats were held less accountable for the war compared to military officers and politicians. "While over 79 percent of the purges involved military circles and 16 percent involved the political world, only less than 1 percent touched the bureaucrats" (Kerbo and McKinstry 1995, 86). According to Baerwald (1959), only "145 members of the senior civil service" were actually removed (82). Second, the GHQ suffered from a shortage of skilled manpower to run the government in the aftermath of the war and the purge, so bureaucrats could not vastly be replaced by a new pool of human resources. The "occupation rule was carried out through the existing bureaucratic organizations. Under these circumstances the traditional bureaucracy returned almost unblemished to its former position of power" (Valeo and Morrison 1983, 80).

All in all, the purge could have been more terrifying. The purge could have been a critical break point for a departure from the prewar legacies if the criminals and collaborators had not been readily released. The *soft* purge meant the Japanese government contained many prewar elements in terms of structure, process, and personnel. As a result, the Occupation did not cut the connection between prewar and postwar; on the contrary, the continuity was sustained, supposedly until today. Ironically, the purge strengthened the power of the Japanese bureaucracy. Because the other groups that had exercised power in prewar and wartime Japan—the military and financial cliques (Gunbatsu and Zaibatsu)—were dismantled by the Occupation authorities, the bureaucracy's power position actually improved after the Japanese defeat in World War II (Koh 1989).

Institutional Reinforcement III: Collapse of the 1955 System

After the GHQ left, Japanese were busy reestablishing their country by their own hands. The LDP as the government party of almost the whole postwar Japan described the early postwar period:

> In the decade from the end of the War to the Conservative Alliance and the formation of the Liberal Democratic Party in 1955, Japan's economic, social, and political structures underwent dramatic change in response to rapid democratization and shifts in Occupation policies. The struggle to cope with these changes continued even after the conclusion of the Peace Treaty in 1951 as great efforts were made to recover from the aftereffects of Occupation politics. This period of

"Preparation," then, can aptly be described as one in which the country struggled to cope with the often painful changes that accompanied the establishment of democratic rule. . . . The political scene remained extremely fluid as political purges ordered by the General Headquarters of the Allied Forces (GHQ) and other forms of intervention in Japanese politics continued.[21]

In 1955, the LDP (自由民主党: Liberal Democratic Party) was created after the historical Conservative Alliance (保守合同) between the Liberty Party (自由党, 1950–1955) and the Japan Democratic Party (日本民主党, 1954–1955). Since then, the LDP has dominated Japanese politics. That is why the postwar Japanese political system is referred to as the 1955 system (55年体制: gojūgonen taisei). The LDP solely constituted the majority in the Diet by having about two times more seats than the Japanese Socialist Party (日本社会党: JSP), the major opposition party. There were only two times the LDP lost majority: 11 months between 1993 and 1994 and 3 years between 2009 and 2012. This section will explore those two brief periods to evaluate if there was a discontinuity to institutional development in Japanese politics.

LDP out of Power: 1993–1994

Numerous scandals involving its members, long-awaited reform programs, and factional rivalries within the party had led to the downfall in 1993 of the LDP after ruling 38 years, and this year is referred to as "the collapse of 1955 System". Nonetheless, in 1994, the LDP strived to regain its power and formed a coalition with the JSP and the New Party Sakigake (新党さ きがけ, Shintō Sakigake).[22] The LDP overcame the crisis by forming alliances with parties with different political stances so as to get back into the government. The alliance turned out to be successful, as they were able to control the House again until 2009. On that account, scholars argue whether the LDP rule ended in 1993 (Kenji 2014). It is viewed as 'an end' by those who pay attention to the fact that it was the LDP's first time being removed from the government. Still, it took only 11 months for the LDP to return, and the short leave did not essentially change the way the government and politics work.

DPJ in Power: 2009–2012

There are some scholars who argue that the year 2009, not 1993, marked "the collapse of the 1955 system", when the LDP lost not only the majority but even plurality in the general election. As the Democratic Party of Japan (民主党: DPJ) had controlled the Upper House since 2007, now both Houses fell under non-LDP rule for the first time in postwar Japanese politics. The DPJ, however, lacked management skills, especially in controlling the bureaucracy, which had become used to a symbiotic relationship with the LDP for most of the postwar period. The dissension between politics and bureaucracy resulted in policy failures. Most notably, the DPJ was heavily criticized for its maladministration with regard to the Fukushima disaster in 2011. All in all, the DPJ ended up making the public believe they were less competent than the LDP, and it eventually led to their defeat in the 2012 general election.

This time it took 3 years, but the LDP returned to government once again. This has reheated the debate over "when, or whether, the 1955 system has collapsed", as the LDP came back with more strength, which was signified by Prime Minister Abe Shinzō and his policy platform with a strong drive. "In this light, the DPJ's failed attempt at a politician-led government offers an interesting example of a critical juncture that eventually did not lead to a durable institutional change" (Zakowski 2015, 3).

LDP Back in Power Since 2012

The Japanese government changed outright after the LDP's victory in the 2012 general election. In comparison to the previous three years under the DPJ, it became very different. Abenomics, a program designed to stimulate the economy, was promoted widely from the start by the Abe cabinet. As a result of its rearmament efforts, massive protests spread throughout Japanese society, which was unprecedented. Even so, the Abe cabinet's approval ratings have steadily risen and have reached 60% (Kyōdō News 2016), allowing it to move forward even further.

The return of the LDP government implies that the old way of Japanese politics has also returned. The DPJ's policy failures are largely attributed to their dissonance with the bureaucracy. The LDP brought back the old gadgets and processes in policy making. On this account, again, there is room for discussion on whether the 1955 system collapsed. There have been ups and downs in their electoral fate, but overall, the LDP's power did not fade away. Neither did the power of bureaucracy.

Conclusion: The Blurring of Politics and Bureaucracy and Seikai-Tensin

In summary, there has been ambiguity with regard to the nature of the decision-making process: whether it's more top-down or bottom-up. First, there is a debate on whether one should put more emphasis on the formal part (i.e., the ringi system) or the informal part (i.e., nemawashi) of decision-making taking place in Japan. Formality would suggest bottom-up, whereas informality would go with top down. Second, in addition to the existing ambivalence, there is temporal variance. At one time, it was actually close to bottom-up, but at other times, it could be more top-down, depending on the power dynamics within the organization.[23] In that regard, the nature of Japanese decision-making is indeed ambiguous. Japanese decision-making is a combination of bottom-up (on the front) and top-down (on the back) processes. The blending of top-down and bottom-up decision-making is highly associated with the blurring of politics and bureaucracy. This explains the complexity with which Japanese politics and the government have worked since the Tokugawa family ruled the country.

This chapter examines centralization and bureaucratization that are deeply embedded in Japanese history and culture. The Tokugawa regime is widely known as a feudal (decentralized) system operated by the samurai as the warrior class, but unlike popular belief, during the Pax Tokugawa of 250 years, it maintained a centralized governance system with the samurai as bureaucrats working within the government. Accordingly, its decision-making process largely revolved around top-down processes at its core, although it may seem bottom-up on the surface.

The traditional elements of centralization and bureaucratization became even more fortified in modern times despite critical junctures that could have weakened them. At the time of the Meiji Reformation, which marks *the* beginning of the modern Japanese state, the Japanese founding fathers progressively adopted modern institutions from western countries to build a modern state. They were largely the samurai, who were both warriors and bureaucrats under the Tokugawa regime. Over the course of early modernization, the state apparatuses and relevant institutions (e.g., educational system) were centralized and equipped with bureaucratic procedures.

In brief, this chapter examines Japanese politics and administration in terms of their centralization and bureaucratization. Through centralization, the central government has come to acquire substantial influence and authority, while bureaucratization has constructed an institutional foundation that bureaucrats can assume critical roles not only in policy implementation but in policy making over a broad range. This has led to the blurring of politics and bureaucracy, which in turn affected individual elites and institutional development in politics and bureaucracy.

The following chapters will uncover the formation and development of Seikai-Tensin based on these historical and cultural accounts. In effect, bureaucrats and politicians work across the bureaucracy and the legislature, and it is believed that their official positions do not matter much as long as they deal with policy matters. This was rather fortified under the long-lasting 1955 system largely because of symbiotic collaborations between the LDP and ministries, both of which control the whole national governance system with highly centralized measures. Differently put, the one-party rule by the LDP implies that the bureaucracy (can) play a key role in policy making under a centralized political administrative system. For example, the LDP works in tandem with the government by having internal organizations, Policy Affairs Research Councils (PARCs, 政務調査会), which all match actual ministries in the government. That is, politicians and bureaucrats all together are thought to be a group of policy makers. Ultimately, this has created conditions in which they both are recognized and respected as the elite who can promote public interests. In this context, it is no wonder, especially to the Japanese people, that former bureaucrats transform themselves into politicians, or Seikai-Tensin. Centralization and bureaucratization provide a base for the formation of the elite with an *amphibious* nature, being politicians *and* bureaucrats.

Notes

1 This is evident in another name for the Tokugawa period, Sakoku (鎖国), meaning a closed country. No outsiders were allowed into Japan, and no Japanese were allowed to exit either.

2 "The perception of new purposes for old practices and tools" (Padgett and McLean 2006, 1506).

3 Kan (官) is bureaucrats, son (尊) is to respect, min (民) is the people, and pi (卑) is to despise.

4 That being said, "[c]rucial to the 'civilization' of the samurai was their education in Confucianism, which was actively promoted, through the foundation of 'fief' schools, as an appropriate ideology for a more orderly society. The Confucianist values of obedience, respect for authority, self-restraint and education facilitated the bureaucratization of the Samurai and legitimated stratification of Tokugawa society" (Fulcher 1988, 231). Nonetheless, "it is important to be aware of the difference between Chinese and Japanese Confucianism. As Bellah (1957, 178–192) and Morishima (1982, 6) have shown, political loyalty was the supreme virtue of Japanese Confucianism. This is not surprising, given Japan's feudal past and the strength of the personal bond between a warrior leader and his followers" (Morishima 1982, 233).

5 The majority of the literature argues that premodern China and Korea had a more centralized and bureaucratic aspect, as they were not feudal societies and had bureaucracies based on meritocracy. On the other hand, there is also an argument that Japan, in substantial terms, may have been more centralized and bureaucratic than those two countries.

6 The bakufu government was the central government located in Edo (江戸), whereas han governments were local governments located in major cities throughout the country. At the top of the former, the shogun from the Tokugawa period resided, while daimyō ruled their own fiefs.

7 "Rank acquisition and promotion was based partly on an individual's performance in official examinations, following the Chinese example. But in contrast to the Chinese system, the Japanese bureaucracy paid considerable attention to family status as a determinant of ranking. Side by side with the examination system, for example was the 'shadow-rank' (*on'i*) system" (Lebra 1993, 33). "For example, if an official enjoyed the first court rank, his son at age twenty-one automatically was given the fifth court rank and his grandson the sixth. The shadow rank thus obtained could, depending on one's father's status, be higher than the rank one might attain by passing qualifying examinations (Miller 1978, 108–109). Furthermore, the Daigakyuryō (Bureau of Great Learning), which trained the examination candidates, was open only to certain professional families and to families of the fifth rank or higher (Kasumi Kaikan 1966, 18)" (cited from Lebra 1993, 34).

8 In this book, samurai (without an article) signifies an abstract image of the warrior class, including cultural aspects, as in its everyday use. *The samurai* (with a definitive article) specifically indicates the warrior class per se.

9 Sankin-Kōtai is distinctive but not unique. King Louis XIV of France also forced the French nobility to reside in his palace at Versailles for six months of each year. Notably, his purpose behind this hostage system was essentially identical to the Japanese one to militarily demobilize them, as a particular emphasis was also put on warrior nobility, that is, *noblesse d'épée* (Nobles of the Sword). This system helped Louis XIV and his successors to establish an absolute monarchy that nullified a prior aristocratic rule, and thus France became a centralized state. Nonetheless, Sankin-Kōtai is still very distinctive in that it lasted for the most of the Tokugawa regime, whereas the French system only lasted for a much shorter time until the French Revolution. Initially, it was required for tozama daimyō in 1635, and then for fudai daimyō in 1642; both began not so long after the inception of the regime and remained effective until its end.

10 Nevertheless, there were discrepancies that were not intended by the system's designer. To begin with, despite the shogunate's efforts to distribute lands to their vassals according to their preferences (i.e., lands with higher kokudaka to more loyal vassals), as stated, the material wealth and class status of a domain did not always match up. In addition, kokudaka was a universal measure to evaluate their gross potential income, as it was also used for a domain in which rice is not a main crop. In such cases, other produce was converted to equivalent koku in terms of their cash value.

11 Meiji is the name of the emperor enthroned in 1868. The Japanese calendar years are named after the incumbent emperor, and historical periods, especially after 1868, take their names from the incumbent emperor of the time (e.g., Meiji, Taishō, Shōwa, and Heisei). A period ends when the emperor dies and thus leaves the throne. As such, the Meiji period lasted from 1868 to 1912.

12 Silberman (1964) states, "the backgrounds of 253 of the 312 men who came to hold high office in the new Japanese central government in the five-year period between early 1868 and early 1873" (2).

13 Or some would argue that a collapse of absolute monarchy was brought about by modernization.

14 This, however, changed over time. "By 1889 Japan's political leaders did not have to look to the ancient Nara period to find justification for political reforms.

The Meiji Restoration was itself beginning to become history and the Meiji Restoration state had started to create its own traditions" (Mehl 1998, 34–35).

15 This double-sided ambiguity can be found in many aspects of Japanese politics and society, as McVeigh (1998), in his study on Japanese society, differentiates an "expressive cultural rituality (e.g., consensus, cooperation, harmony, loyalty, and ritualized behavior) and an 'instrumental' economic rationality (e.g., control, coordination, management, compulsion, and regulated behavior). Another way to state this is that Japanese sociopolitical patterns reveal the rituality in rationalism and the rationality in ritualism" (2).

16 The buke in Tōkyō vs. the kuge in Kyōto can also be an example of duality in the governance system, which also concurrently disappeared in the Meiji period.

17 Takane (1976) analyzes samples of the national leadership in the years 1860 (207 men), 1890 (202 men), 1920 (331 men), 1936 (393 men), and 1969 (445 men) against variables of inherited status, political career of the father, regional origin, and education level.

18 "Yet there is not complete agreement on who to designate as the genrō, even in Japanese scholarship, though the lists do not vary widely. For example, see Hayashi Shigeru's entry under genrō in *Hyakka jiten* (heibon-sha, 1956, x, 38, or Umetani Noboru's chart in *Nihon kindai shi jiten* (1961), p. 161. Professor Oka Yoshitake omits Kuroda from his list in *Kindai Nihon seiji shi* (1962), p. 254" (Hacket 1998, 7).

19 Although it went through "three apparently distinct periods", there was "a continuity of bureaucratic authoritarian politics": "1) the period of bureaucratic oligarchy from 1869 to 1900 during which the bureaucracy led by a small group of men later known as the genrō dominated day-to-day as well long-term policy decisions and implementation; 2) the period of limited pluralism from 1900 to 1936 during which political parties characterized by a narrow ideological range and leadership by ex-bureaucrats participated in policy making; and, 3) 1936 to 1945, the period of civil-military bureaucratic technocratic domination of policy making and implementation" (Silberman 1978, 385–388).

20 Much of the drafting was done by two senior army officers with law degrees: Milo Rowell and Courtney Whitney, although others chosen by MacArthur had a large say in the document as well (Dower 1999, 365–367).

21 "A History of the Liberal Democratic Party—Before th[e] Conservative Alliance" (Liberal Democratic Party n.d.)

22 The New Party Sakigake was split from the LDP right before the 1993 general election.

23 More specifically, when politicians are more powerful, the decision-making process tends to be more top-down, and vice versa. Accordingly, as the power of the cabinet grew in recent years, the decision-making process has become more top-down than before—this will be discussed at length in the later chapters.

Works Cited

Baerwald, Hans H. (1959). *The Purge of Japanese Leaders under the Occupation.* (Berkeley: University of California Press).

Beasley, W. G. (1963). *The Modern History of Japan.* (New York and London: Frederick A. Praeger).

Bellah, Robert N. (1957). *Tokugawa Religion.* (Glencoe: The Free Press).

Brown, D. M. (1988). The Cambridge History of Japan (Vol. 1). J. W. Hall, D. H. Shively, W. H. McCullough, Y. Kozo, M. B. Jansen, & P. Duus (eds.). (Cambridge: Cambridge University Press).

Burton, Gene, and Manab Thakur (1998). *Management Today: Principles And Practice*. (New Delhi: Tata McGraw-Hill Education).

Capoccia, Giovanni, and R. Daniel Kelemen (2007). "The Study of Critical Junctures: Theory, Narrative, and Counterfactuals in Historical Institutionalism," *World Politics*, 59(3): 341–369.

Cortell, A. P., and S. Peterson (1999). "Altered States: Explaining Domestic Institutional Change," *British Journal of Political Science*, 29(1): 177–203.

Craig, Albert M. (1986). "Chapter 2: Central Government," *Japan in Transition: From Tokugawa to Meiji*, pp. 36–67. M. B. Jansen and G. Rozman (eds.). (Princeton, NJ: Princeton University Press).

Donnelly, Paul, and John Hogan (2012). "Understanding Policy Change Using a Critical Junctures Theory in Comparative Context: The Cases of Ireland and Sweden," *Policy Studies Journal*, 40(2): 324–350.

Dower, John W. (1999). *Embracing Defeat: Japan in the Wake of World War II* (1st ed.). (New York: W.W. Norton & Co/New Press).

Dower, John W., and Hirata Tetsuo (2007). "Japan's Red Purge: Lessons from a Saga of Suppression of Free Speech and Thought," *The Asia-Pacific Journal*, 5(7): 1–7.

Fulcher, James (1988). "The Bureaucratization of the State and the Rise of Japan," *British Journal of Sociology*, 39(2): 228–254.

Hackett, R. F. (1998). "Chapter 1: Political Modernization and the Meiji Genrō," *Meiji Japan (Vol. III): The Mature Meiji State*, pp. 3–24. (New York: Rutledge).

Higley, J., and M. Burton (2006). *Elite Foundations of Liberal Democracy*. (Lanham: Rowman & Littlefield Publishers).

Kasumi Kaikan霞會館 (1966). *History of Kazoku Association* 『華族會館史』. (Kyoto: Kasumi Kaikan Kyoto Branch 霞會館京都支部). (Written in Japanese).

Katsuta, Seiji勝田政治 (2002). *MHA and Formation of the Meiji State* 『内務省と明治国家形成』. (Tokyo: YoshikawaKobunkan吉川弘文館). (Written in Japanese).

Kerbo, Harold R., and John A. McKinstry (1995). *Who Rules Japan?: The Inner Circles of Economic and Political Power*. (New York: Greenwood Publishing Group).

Koh, B. C. (1989). *Japan's Administrative Elite*. (Berkeley: University of California Press).

Krauss, Ellis S., and Robert J. Pekkanen (2010). "The Rise and Fall of Japan's Liberal Democratic Party," *Journal of Asian Studies*, 69(1): 5–15.

Kyōdō News (2016). "Survey Finds Abe Cabinet Support Rate Surges to 60.7%," www.japantimes.co.jp/news/2016/11/27/national/politics-diplomacy/abe-cabinet-support-rate-surges-60-7/#.WF-M46J95sM (last accessed September 1, 2022).

Lebra, Takie S. (1993). *Above the Clouds: Status Culture of the Modern Japanese Nobility*. (Berkeley: University of California Press).

Liberal Democratic Party (n.d.). "A History of the Liberal Democratic Party: Before th(e) Conservative Alliance," www.jimin.jp/english/about-ldp/history/104228. html (last accessed September 1, 2022).

Mahoney, James (2000). "Path Dependence in Historical Sociology," *Theory and Society*, 29(4): 507–548.

McVeigh, Brian J. (1998). *The Nature of the Japanese State: Rationality and Rituality*. (New York: Routledge).

Mehl, Margaret (1998). "Chapter 3: Tradition as Justification for Change: History in the Service of the Japanese Government," In *Meiji Japan (Vol. II): The Growth of the Meiji State*, pp. 28–35. Peter Francis Kornicki (ed.). (New York: Rutledge).

Miller, Richard J. (1978). *Japan's First Bureaucracy: A Study of Eighth Century Government*. (Ithaca: Cornell University East Asia Program).

Morishima, Michio (1982). *Why Has Japan 'Succeeded'?: Western Technology and Japanese Ethos*. (Cambridge: Cambridge University Press).

Padgett, John F., and Paul D. McLean (2006). "Organizational Invention and Elite Transformation: The Birth of Partnership Systems in Renaissance Florence," *American Journal of Sociology*, 111(5): 1463–1568.

Park, Hoon 박훈 (2014). *How Could Meiji Ishin Be Possible?* 메이지 유신은 어떻게 가능했는가. (Seoul: Mineumsa 서울: 민음사). (Written in Korean).

Schoppa, Leonard J. (2011). "Path Dependence in the Evolution of Japan's Party System since 1993," In *The Evolution of Japan's Party System: Politics and Policy in an Era of Institutional Change*. Leonard J. Schoppa (ed.). (Toronto: University of Toronto Press).

Silberman, Bernard S. (1964). *Ministers of Modernization: Elite Mobility in the Meiji Restoration, 1868–1873*. (Tucson: University of Arizona Press).

——— (1967). "Bureaucratic Development and the Structure of Decision-Making in the Meiji Period: The Case of the Genrō," *Journal of Asian Studies*, 27(1): 81–94.

——— (1973). "Ringisei: Traditional Values or Organizational Imperatives in the Japanese Upper Civil Service, 1868–1945," *Journal of Asian Studies*, 32(2): 251–264.

——— (1978). "Bureaucratic Development and Bureaucratization: The Case of Japan," *Social Science History*, 2(4): 385–398.

Takane, Masaaki 高根正昭 (1976). *Japanese Political Elites: Modernization and Quantitative Analyses* 『日本の政治エリート—近代化と数量分析』. (Tokyo: ChuoKoronShinsha中央公論新社). (Written in Japanese).

Uwajima City History and Culture Lecture Series (2011). "宇和島伊達家の参勤交代,"（第19回 宇和島市民歴史文化講座「そこ・どこや」 2011年1月16日). (Written in Japanese).

Valeo, Francis Ralph, and Charles Edward Morrison. (1983). "Chapter 5: The Diet and the Bureaucracy: The Budget as a Case Study," In *The Japanese Diet and the US Congress*. Francis Ralph Valeo and Charles Edward Morrison (eds.). (Boulder: Westview Press).

Watanabe, Hiroshi 渡辺浩. (2010). *Early Modern Japanese Society and Neo-Confucianism*『近世日本社会と宋学』. (Tokyo: University of Tokyo Press東京大学出版会). (Written in Japanese).

Westney, Dorothy Eleanor. (1987). *Imitation and Innovation: The Transfer of Western Organizational Patterns to Meiji Japan*. (Boston: Harvard University Press).

Wilson, Robert A. (1957). *Genesis of the Meiji Government in Japan, 1868–1871.* (Berkeley: University of California Press).

Woodall, Brian (2014). *Growing Democracy in Japan: The Parliamentary Cabinet System Since 1868.* (Lexington: University Press of Kentucky).

Zakowski, Karol. (2015). *Decision-Making Reform in Japan: The DPJ's Failed Attempt at a Politician-Led Government.* (New York: Routledge).

3 Self-Transforming Elites

Seikai-Tensin's Election to the Diet

Introduction

For Seikai-Tensin politicians, personal background is an essential component of their identity. By definition, Seikai-Tensin politicians are "former bureaucrats" who passed highly competitive exams and who likely graduated from a prestigious university. Thus, studies on their electoral success should primarily investigate their personal backgrounds, which are acquired through their abilities and endeavors, in lieu of merely focusing on systematic aspects of election. Nevertheless, this book does not overlook structures, institutions, and/or systems in explaining the Seikai-Tensin phenomenon. Rather, this book posits individuals are constrained by institutions surrounding them, and in turn, institutions are shaped by individuals. Thus, one's personal background is an output of personal as well as social factors in that individuals develop and utilize a background constrained by various institutions. For example, in the case of Seikai-Tensin, personal behavior would be reinforced by culture that values elite qualities.

As such, this book uses a relaxed definition of institutions to indicate both formal and informal ones. As formal institutions, this book encompasses the whole Japanese political system consisting of governmental institutions and political process, such as bureaucracy, the Diet, the cabinet, elections, and political parties. In addition, the educational system (i.e., the Escalator School System and competitive college entrance exams; refer to endnote 3 of Chapter 5) is also included within formal institutions. Informal institutions refers to culture, practices, and norms *within* and/or *surrounding* the aforementioned formal institutions. More importantly, the elite structures and networks constitute an important part of informal institutions, implicitly having an enormous influence on actors' behavior. In short, this chapter will largely draw on and contribute to studies on a variety of formal and informal institutions in politics, bureaucracy, and society. Eventually, this chapter will be a critical addition to the existing literature on the elite (i.e., elite recruitment and

DOI: 10.4324/9781003319207-3

elite networks), political behavior with regard to elections (i.e., candidate quality and vote choice), and political institutions (i.e., relationship between the bureaucracy and the legislature).

Electoral Outcomes and Candidates' Attributes

Regarding election results, candidate considerations are clearly one of the important factors (Glass 1985, 519). Campbell et al. (1960) divide the electorate into three groups: party voters, policy voters, and candidate voters. Party and issue-oriented explanations have received extensive scholarly attention. For instance, many have assumed that party identification plays a more critical role in voters' decisions in election than individual candidates' attributes (Richardson 1988). Beginning with Stokes (1966), however, attention has been directed toward candidates as well. The emergence of a particularly attractive candidate, or the existence of a somewhat unattractive candidate, has a great impact on voting decisions (Kelley and Mirer 1974; Popkin et al. 1976; Markus and Converse 1979).

Cain et al. (1987) conceptualize "the personal vote", which refers to a candidate's electoral support originating in his or her "personal qualities, qualifications, activities and record". The part of the vote that is not personal includes "support for the candidate based on his or her partisan affiliation, fixed voter characteristics such as the state of economy, and performance evaluations centered on the head of the governing party" (Cain et al. 1987, 9).

Notwithstanding the aforementioned structural view in the mainstream, a few studies also view Japanese election outcomes from the "personal vote" perspective (McCubbins and Rosenbluth 1995). Following the tradition of personal vote research elsewhere, they posit structural factors as a primary cause inducing the personal vote. Within multi-member districts (MMDs), which have been a primary part of the postwar Japanese electoral system, a candidate who finds himself/herself in danger of losing is much better off trying to convince people who already support his/her party to change from one candidate to another than trying to convince those who support the opposition to switch parties. If the key to victory is attracting voters who already support their party, issue- or party-based strategies would not be very effective. As a result, each candidate has to build up his or her own personal vote because he or she cannot wholly depend on party vote to get him or her elected (Reed 1994). As such, formal institutions such as structures and systems induce "personalizing effects", which in turn have politicians seek the personal vote (Crisp et al. 2004).

To acquire "the personal vote", politicians offer various constituency services through franking, visits, casework, and so on (Cain et al. 1984).

Japanese congresspeople also provide people with such constituency services, yet in a much costlier way, vigorously relying upon political contributions collected and distributed by the party leadership, individual political
funds spent through kōenkai (後援会) during election campaigns, and
pork—expenditures by the government that aim to benefit constituents of
a politician in exchange for support during a campaign or for their vote—
distributed throughout a representative's legislative tenure (Cox and Thies
2000). By way of illustration,

> LDP politicians and their minions show up at weddings and funerals
> with money in their pockets. They sponsor flower-arranging classes
> [生け花教室: ikebana-kyōshitsu], local festivals [祭り: matsuri], trips
> to hot springs [温泉旅行: onsen-ryokō], and all sorts of other activities
> that connect name recognition with goodwill in their districts.
>
> (Rosenbluth and Thies 2010, x; past tense in
> the original text has been changed to present tense)

   All in all, the more money a candidate collects, spends, and attracts, the
more likely s/he is to be elected.[1] Yet "another possible basis of a personal
vote is personal attributes and characteristics of the representative that
are largely divorced from either district service or policy positions" (Herrera and Yawn 1999). The more qualified a politician is, the more likely
s/he is to be perceived as being competent; his/her posited competence,
inferred from personal background as a voting cue, would ensure constituents believed their representative would bring more benefits using his/her
ability, experiences, and connections (Carson et al. 2007). Nonetheless,
politicians' qualities, including background and experiences, have not been
given due attention either in the personal vote literature or in Japanese studies; as such, "the personal vote in Japan" has not been much highlighted
by research.
   Among others, educational and occupational background, which are so
interrelated with each other, are prominent in deciding who is elite and
who is not, especially in Japan. Most Seikai-Tensin politicians, if not all,
graduate from one of the top universities in the nation, which greatly helps
them pass a civil-service examination, which in turn helps them successfully acquire a post-bureaucratic job in politics. Voters will support former bureaucrats because they believe that they will be most successful at
"bringing home the bacon" using well-established networks acquired while
in the bureaucracy (Steinmo 2010, 102, footnote 22). With bounded rationality and time constraints, however, voters do not make a decision based
on perfect information on candidates; especially, it is hard to follow up
their representatives' legislative performance over the course of legislative

terms. Most Japanese legislation is proposed by the government, which renders bill sponsorship unreliable in evaluating a legislator's achievement. To compensate for limited information, voters tend to count on heuristics such as a candidate's personal background to reason about his/her competence (Popkin et al. 1976). In Japan, personal background matters more than any other qualifications, probably due to *elitism* ingrained in its culture and history.

Political science research provides insights regarding the electoral advantages of bureaucratic backgrounds, which are held by Seikai-Tensin politicians. A bureaucratic background might have a *direct* effect under the assumption of perfect information or, more realistically, have a *symbolic* impact under imperfect information or bounded rationality. Seikai-Tensin politicians' *substantial* competence such as expertise and networks is important with regard to vote choice, but ordinary citizens might not have sufficient resources (i.e., time, money, and perfect rationality) to access and process the information regarding candidate quality. In such situations with imperfect information and bounded rationality, voters make a decision using heuristics like a candidate's personal background (Popkin 1994). Either way—perfect or imperfect information—bureaucratic background is presumed to have an influence on vote choice and thus Seikai-Tensin politicians' election to the Diet.

This chapter will explore the effects of the most personal basis of "the personal vote"—personal attributes acquired prior to entering politics—on Seikai-Tensin politicians' election. The predominance of candidate attributes in the Japanese voter's decision-making process presents a fine testing ground for this argument. Because of the electoral system (i.e., multi-member district (MMD) with single non-transferable vote (SNTV)), which allows multiple candidates from the same party to run in a district, Japanese elections have evolved around fiercely competitive campaign strategies based on personal favors and pork-barrel politics. One cannot deny that the clientelistic characteristics of Japanese electoral politics have become so firmly embedded that candidates and constituents rigidly continue to cultivate their private connections, exchanging votes and benefits.

This tendency toward candidate-oriented money politics has somewhat weakened since the electoral system reform in 1996, as the Lower House electoral districts turned into single member districts (SMDs).[2] In the aftermath of the reform, the relationship between voters and parties abated, and party organizations' mobilizing power also diminished (Taniguchi 2004). Hamamoto (2007) argues for "the decline of personal vote" by adducing descriptive statistics and survey results as evidence: 1) large parties' increasing dominance in SMDs (i.e., winner-takes-all), 2) decline in kōenkai and interest groups' influence, and 3) decrease in voters' interests in regionalism. In other words, voting behavior has become more party oriented as evaluation of the prime minister and Cabinet become more influential (Hirano 2008). Nevertheless, candidate-oriented campaign strategies such as pork barrel politics are still effective in Japanese general elections (Natori 2002). Kōenkai, even after the reform, functions as a crucial campaigning tool for parties and politicians (Yamada 1997; Park 2000; Taniguchi 2004; Krauss and Pekkanen 2004). Not only the LDP's but the DPJ's election campaigns revolve around individualistic tactics (Mori and Tsutsumi 2010; Teruya 2010). Interestingly, veteran legislators from the LDP appear to have increased their district activities under the new electoral system (Hamamoto and Nemoto 2011). As a consequence, many scholars have observed that Japanese voters prefer personal voting to party voting despite reformers' attempts to make Japanese electoral politics party oriented (Miyake 2001; Tsutsumi 2009; Natori 2014). This is in part also because vote choice made upon evaluation of individual politicians continues, as the House of Councillors continues to operate upon MMD and open proportional representation (PR) system. All in all, candidates still should make every effort to claim what they have "personally" done and/or can do for their own constituencies in order to continuously get reelected.

Moreover, despite the strong party effects due to the LDP's prolonged one-party dominance for decades, candidate factors seem to be prominent. The party leadership also prefers to recruit politicians with good quality, which will eventually increase the probability of winning them seats in the parliament. Seikai-Tensin politicians are considered viable candidates, especially given that political parties recruit young bureaucrats at senior levels despite their short bureaucratic experience and expertise. They are on the fast track eligible for a promotion toward top levels. These qualifications per se render them sufficiently competent. This explains why political parties do not expect political experience and/or training for retired bureaucrats before fielding them in elections. As such, political elite recruitment from the pool of bureaucratic elites is not uncommon in Japan, and it has led to the rise of Seikai-Tensin politicians, which has given rise to interactions between and an integration of bureaucratic and political elites. In fact, the fusing of relationships and relative power of bureaucrats and politicians in policymaking has been at the heart of most interpretations of postwar Japanese politics (Muramatsu and Krauss 1984, 128).

Seikai-Tensin's Political Success and Electoral Process

Figure 3.1 summarizes the main processes by which Seikai-Tensin politicians transform themselves into politicians through elections. They first need to develop their primary qualifications such as a diploma from a prestigious educational institution and a state certificate passing the Type I civil service

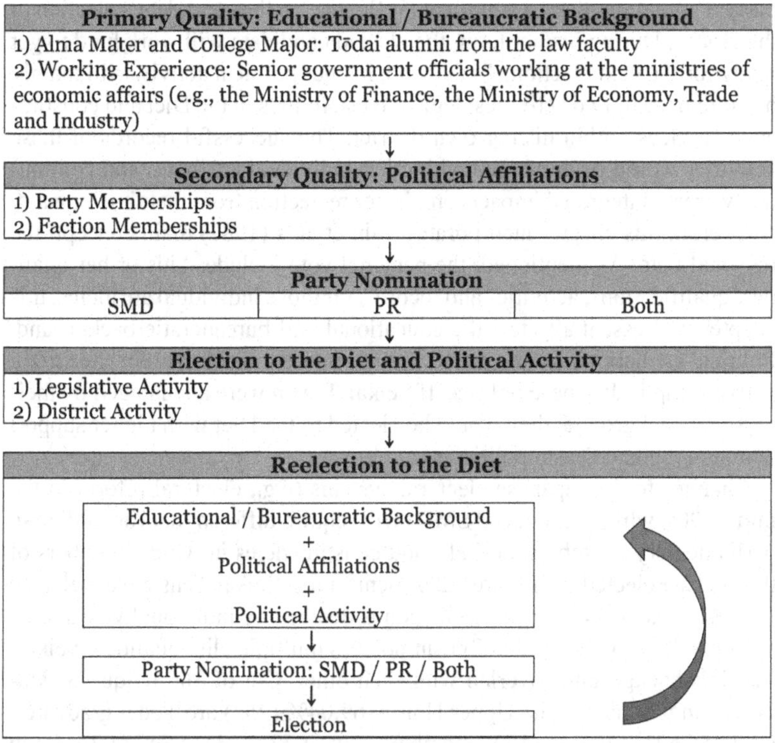

Primary Quality: Educational / Bureaucratic Background
1) Alma Mater and College Major: Tōdai alumni from the law faculty
2) Working Experience: Senior government officials working at the ministries of economic affairs (e.g., the Ministry of Finance, the Ministry of Economy, Trade and Industry)

↓

Secondary Quality: Political Affiliations
1) Party Memberships
2) Faction Memberships

↓

Party Nomination		
SMD	PR	Both

↓

Election to the Diet and Political Activity
1) Legislative Activity
2) District Activity

↓

Reelection to the Diet

Educational / Bureaucratic Background
+
Political Affiliations
+
Political Activity
↓
Party Nomination: SMD / PR / Both
↓
Election

Figure 3.1 Seikai-Tensin's Electoral Process

examination. Competent university graduates begin their bureaucratic careers from the central government. Their educational and bureaucratic backgrounds serve as useful credentials in the transformation. Using their educational and bureaucratic background, bureaucrats, at a relatively young age, retire from the government and join major political parties and influential political factions within. Political memberships matter primarily because a political party is a group of politicians with close personal connections to each other, working together toward a shared goal: getting reelected, creating good policy, and pursuing successful political careers.

In the party nomination, the party leadership, consisting of powerful faction leaders, consider these political affiliations along with individual educational and bureaucratic background. Since it is acceptable to simultaneously nominate a candidate for a SMD and PR seat, the party can support the candidate to its greatest extent by fielding him/her for both. In addition, if his/her rank on the PR list is high, we can assume that the party is very much willing to have him/her elected. All these aforementioned factors, such as educational and bureaucratic background, political affiliations, and party nomination, exert a significant influence on the candidate's election to the House. During his/her term, the elected candidate will work hard to get ready for the next election. To that end, his/her political activity will mainly be composed of two activities: legislative activities in the Diet and constituency services within his/her own district. The successful records of these activities would be combined with other individual attributes and continuously create integrated impacts on his/her reelection from that time onward.

Overall, this chapter incorporates Cain et al.'s (1987) main concept: the personal vote. As mentioned, the personal vote includes "his or her qualities, qualifications, activities and record". Of those individual attributes, this chapter will essentially test the educational and bureaucratic background. Political affiliations will be tested as well in order to control for the strong partisanship in Japanese politics. If Seikai-Tensin were advantaged by their personal background, they would be elected to the Diet with higher support than non–Seikai-Tensin politicians.

Changes to the Japanese electoral systems (e.g., electoral reform in the mid-1990s, which introduced SMD) will require different data according to parliamentary chambers, periods, and constituencies in which members of the Diet are elected. As Figure 3.2 presents, most Seikai-Tensin were elected from MMDs or SMDs, where election is decided by individual vote share.

Many, if not most, Seikai-Tensin possess multiple elite qualities. Seikai-Tensin's backgrounds overlap with each other. Out of 365 unique Seikai-Tensin individuals in the Upper House, 69.04% (252) are Tōdai graduates, while 55.62% (203) are LDP members. Out of 572 unique Seikai-Tensin in the Lower House, 40.61% (294) are Tōdai graduates, while 47.20% (270) are LDP members. It is worth noting that a Tōdai background would be useful when combined with a bureaucratic or political background or both.

On the contrary, legislative performance does not seem to have a meaningful influence on Japanese elections. It does not greatly change the size and significance of the main independent variables. Tables 3.1 and 3.2 corroborate these results. The two tables show the results of t-tests that compare the means of each group in the House of Councillors and House of Representatives, respectively. The two tables reflect the changes of electoral systems by period.

For example, Table 3.1 shows that the number of reelections of Seikai-Tensin councillors with bureaucratic backgrounds, on average, are 0.18 times greater than those of non–Seikai-Tensin throughout the postwar period (1947–2013), and the differences are statistically significant at the 0.05 level until 2001. LDP membership also turns out to be helpful in one's reelection to the Upper House. In the most recent period (2001–2013), the advantages of being Seikai-Tensin seem to disappear, but we cannot be sure of it, because the differences are not statistically significant. In Table 3.2,

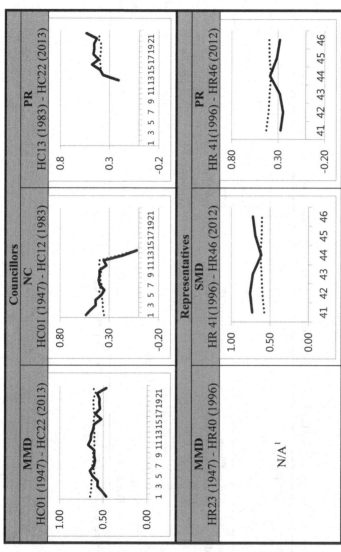

X-axis: Legislative Session Y-axis: Proportion of Diet Members
—— Seikai-Tensin   ······ Non–Seikai-Tensin

Figure 3.2 Electoral Districts of Seikai-Tensin

Table 3.1 Personal Background and Differences in the Number of Reelections (House of Councillors)

Background	Group	Difference (p-value)			
		All (1947–2013)	I (1947–1983)	II (1983–2001)	III (2001–2013)
Bureaucratic Background	Seikai-Tensin	0.18 (0.0026)**	0.22 (0.0050)**	0.15 (0.0103)*	−0.12 (0.3378)
	Non–Seikai-Tensin				
Party Affiliation	LDP	0.41 (0.0000)***	0.48 (0.0000)***	0.40 (0.0000)***	−0.21 (0.0589)
	Non-LDP				
Educational Background	Tokyo University Alumni	0.14 (0.0211)	0.07 (0.3490)	0.10 (0.3971)	0.24 (0.0741)
	Non-Tokyo University Alumni				
Sex	Male	0.12 (0.1380)	0.13 (0.3552)	0.22 (0.0812)	0.18 (0.2327)
	Female				

Note: p-values are shown in parentheses; *$p < 0.05$, **$p < 0.01$, ***$p < 0.001$

Table 3.2 Personal Background and Differences in the Number of Reelections (House of Representatives)

Background	Group	Difference (p-value)		
		All (1947–2014)	Before Reform (1947–1996)	After Reform (1996–2014)
Bureaucratic Background	Seikai-Tensin Non–Seikai-Tensin	0.71 (0.0000)***	0.70 (0.0000)***	0.50 (0.0027)**
Party Affiliation	LDP Non-LDP	2.08 (0.0000)***	2.63 (0.0000)***	1.18 (0.0000)***
Educational Background	Tokyo University Alumni Non–Tokyo University Alumni	0.54 (0.0000)***	0.53 (0.0000)***	0.43 (0.0029)**
Sex	Male Female	2.38 (0.0000)***	1.80 (0.0000)***	1.68 (0.0000)***

Note: *p*-values are shown in parentheses ** $p < 0.01$, *** $p < 0.001$.

despite the significant effects of LDP membership, one's bureaucratic background appears to be critical in all periods. In short, elite background holders make a significant difference from others in their tenure in legislative office. In particular, with a bureaucratic background and LDP membership, one is more likely to be reelected, to varying degrees. Seikai-Tensin's multiple elite qualities may help them get elected. Their election can translate to a transformation from bureaucratic to political elite. In that regard, an elite quality begets another one, which all together creates and reshapes an elite.

Conclusion

This chapter examines the electoral advantage enjoyed by Seikai-Tensin politicians with distinguished personal backgrounds. All else being equal, Seikai-Tensin politicians would be likely to receive higher vote shares than non–Seikai-Tensin politicians. Examining the results of the postwar Japanese congressional elections, this chapter makes an attempt to answer the questions: Was there any evidence of the personal vote? Were Seikai-Tensin politicians able to be elected for their bureaucratic and educational backgrounds or something else? Put differently, do their superior backgrounds really benefit Seikai-Tensin politicians in winning an election? After careful scrutiny, answers to those questions turned out to be largely positive. The results suggest that being a former senior bureaucrat and graduate from a prestigious university, namely the University of Tokyo, would actually help a candidate achieve electoral success. The Japanese electoral process revolving around individual candidates, who are backed up by major political parties, would encourage (would-be) Seikai-Tensin politicians to utilize their backgrounds as one of their most valuable political assets.

Notes

1 "Watanabe Michio, a seasoned LDP politician, once quipped that he always had a black tie in one pocket for weddings and a white tie in the other for funerals". In Japan, when we attend funerals or go to the hospital to console patients, it is traditional to bring a big wreath and a cash gift. Nobody gives such a small amount as 1,000 yen or 2,000 yen [$10–$20]. Everybody gives 10,000 or 20,000 yen, and flowers cost another 20,000 yen. . . . People die every day, you know, Diet members . . . say that if they do not attend these, they will lose in the next election" (Rosenbluth and Thies 2010, 56).

2 "Under the current (Lower House electoral) system, called the heiritsu-sei (並立制) or parallel system, the votes for the 300 single member district (hereafter SMD) seats and the 180 proportional representation (hereafter PR) seats remain completely separate, though the fact that candidates may run simultaneously for an SMD and a PR seat does complicate the process somewhat" (Reed 1997). "The voter receives two ballots sequentially: first, the SMD ballot, which is placed in the SMD ballot box, then the process repeats with a PR ballot. When marking the SMD ballot, the voter is provided a list of candidate with their party labels. When marking the PR ballot, the voter is provided only with a list of party labels" (Reed 1999, 257–258).

Works Cited

Cain, Bruce E., John A. Ferejohn, and Morris P. Fiorina (1984). "The Constituency Service Basis of the Personal Vote for U.S. Representatives and British Members of Parliament," *American Political Science Review*, 78(1): 110–125.

―――― (1987). *The Personal Vote: Constituency Service and Electoral Independence*. (Cambridge: Harvard University Press).

Campbell, A., P. E. Converse, W. E. Miller, and D. E. Stokes (1960). *The American Voter*. (New York: Wiley).

Carson, Jamie L., Erik J. Engstrom, and Jason M. Roberts (2007). "Candidate Quality, the Personal Vote, and the Incumbency Advantage in Congress," *American Political Science Review*, 101(2): 289–301.

Cox, G. W., & M. F. Thies (2000). "How Much Does Money Matter? 'Buying' Votes in Japan, 1967–1990," *Comparative Political Studies*, 33(1): 37–57.

Crisp, Brian F., Maria C. Escobar-Lemmon, Bradford S. Jones, Mark P. Jones, and Michelle M. Taylor-Robinson (2004). "Vote: Seeking Incentives and Legislative Representation in Six Presidential Democracies," *Journal of Politics*, 66(3): 823–846.

Glass, David P. (1985). "Evaluating Presidential Candidates: Who Focuses on Their Personal Attributes?," *Public Opinion Quarterly*, 49(4): 517–534.

Hamamoto, Shinshuke 濱本真輔 (2007). "The Decline of Personal Vote「個人投票の低下」," *Review of Electoral Studies*『選挙学会紀要』, 9: 47–66. (Written in Japanese).

Hamamoto, Shinshuke, and Nemoto Kuniaki 濱本真輔・根元邦朗 (2011). "Campaigning for Personal Votes and Its Impact on Electoral Outcomes: How District Activities Lead to Votes (Or Not).「個人中心の再選戦略とその有効性—選挙区活動は得票に結びつくのか?」," *The Annuals of Japanese Political Science Association*『年報政治学』, 62(2): 70–97. (Written in Japanese).

Herrera, Richard, and Michael Yawn (1999). "The Emergence of the Personal Vote," *Journal of Politics*, 61(1): 136–150.

Hirano, Hiroshi 平野浩 (2008). "Changes in the New Government-Voter Relationship in Terms of Voting Behavior「投票行動からみた執政部ー有権者関係の変容」," *Annals of the Japan Association for Comparative Politics Comparative Politics of Leadership* 『比較政治学会年報:リーダーシップの比較政治学』, pp. 19–38. (Written in Japanese).

Kelley, S. Jr., and T. Mirer (1974). "The Simple Act of Voting," *American Political Science Review*, 68(2): 572–591.

Krauss, Ellis S., and Robert J. Pekkanen (2004). "Explaining Party Adaptation to Electoral Reform: The Discreet Charm of the LDP?," *Journal of Japanese Studies*, 30(1): 1–34.

Markus, G. B., and P. E. Converse. (1979). "A Dynamic Simultaneous Equation Model of Equation Model of Electoral Choice," *American Political Science Review*, 73: 1055–1070.

McCubbins, Mathew D., and Frances M. Rosenbluth (1995). "Party Provision for Personal Politics: Dividing the Vote in Japan," In *Structure and Policy in Japan and the United States*. Peter F. Cowhey and Mathew D. McCubbins (eds.). (Cambridge: Cambridge University Press).

Miyake, Ichiro 三宅一郎 (2001). *Electoral Reform and Voting Behavior*『選挙制度変革と投票行動』. (Tokyo: Bokutakusha木鐸社). (Written in Japanese).

Mori, Michiya, and Tsutsumi Hidetaka 森道哉・堤英敬 (2010). "DPJ Candidates' Electoral Campaigns and Competitive Environments「民主党候補者の選挙キャンペーンと競争環境」," In *Politics of Change of Government Election*『政権交代選挙の政治学』. Shiratori Hiroshi (ed.) 白鳥浩編. (Kyoto: MinervaShobo ミネルヴァ書房). (Written in Japanese).

Muramatsu, Michio, and Ellis S. Krauss (1984). "Bureaucrats and Politicians in Policymaking: The Case of Japan," *American Political Science Review*, 78(1): 126–146.

Natori, Ryota 名取良太 (2002). "Electoral System Reform and Pork Barrel Politics「選挙制度改革と利益誘導政治」," *Japanese Journal of Electoral Studies*『選挙研究』, 17: 128–141. (Written in Japanese).

——— (2014). "Party and Personal Voting in the 2012 Japanese Lower House Election 「2012年衆院選における政党投票と候補者投票」," *Journal of Informatics*『情報研究』, 41: 71–84. (Written in Japanese).

Park, Cheol-Hee 朴喆熙 (2000). *How Legislators Are Made: Electoral Strategies in SMDs*『代議士のつくられ方—小選挙区の選挙戦略』. (Tokyo: Bungeishunju 文藝春秋). (Written in Japanese).

Popkin, Samuel L. (1994). *The Reasoning Voter: Communication and Persuasion in Presidential Campaigns*. (Chicago: University of Chicago Press).

Popkin, Samuel L., J. W. Gorman, C. Phillips, and J. A. Smith (1976). "Comment: What Have You Done for Me Lately? Toward an Investment Theory of Voting," *American Political Science Review*, 70(3): 779–805.

Reed, Steven R. (1994). "Democracy and the Personal Vote: A Cautionary Tale from Japan," *Electoral Studies*, 13(1): 17–28.

——— (1997). "The 1996 Japanese General Election," *Electoral Studies*, 16(1): 121–125.

——— (1999). "Strategic Voting in the 1996 Japanese General Election," *Comparative Political Studies*, 32(2): 257–270.

Richardson, Bradley M. (1988). "Constituency Candidates Versus Parties in Japanese Voting Behavior," *American Political Science Review*, 82(3): 695–718.

Rosenbluth, Frances M., and Michael F. Thies (2010). *Japan Transformed: Political and Economic Restructuring*. (Princeton: Princeton University Press).

Steinmo, Sven (2010). *The Evolution of Modern States: Sweden, Japan, and the United States*. (Cambridge: Cambridge University Press).

Stokes, D. E. (1966). "Some Dynamic Elements of Contests for the Presidency," *American Political Science Review*, 60(1): 19–28.

Taniguchi, Masaki 谷口将紀 (2004). *Modern Japan's Electoral Politics: Testing the Electoral Reform*『現代日本の選挙政治—選挙制度改革を検証する—』. (Tokyo: Tokyo University Press東京大学出版会). (Written in Japanese).

Teruya Hiroyuki 照屋寛之 (2010). "Children's Allowances as a Sensation「子ども手当という突風」," In *Politics of Change of Government Election*『政権交代選挙の政治学』. Shiratori Hiroshi (ed.) 白鳥浩編. (Kyoto: MinervaShobo ミネルヴァ書房). (Written in Japanese).

Tsutsumi, Hidetaka 堤英敬 (2009). "Personal Vote in Japan after Electoral Reform「選挙制度改革以降の日本における候補者個人投票」," *Kagawa Law Review*『香川法学』, 29(1): 58–90. (Written in Japanese).

Yamada, Masahiro 山田真裕 (1997). "Influences of Political Reorganization and Electoral Reform in Rural Districts「農村型選挙区における政界再編および選挙制度改革の影響」," In *Research on Political Reorganization: General Elections under the New Electoral System*『政界再編の研究—新選挙制度による総選挙』, pp. 113–142. Otake Hideo (ed.) 大嶽秀夫編. (Tokyo: Yuhikaku有斐閣). (Written in Japanese).

4 Racing to the Top
Seikai-Tensin in the Cabinet

Introduction

Seikai-Tensin's political success can also be found in the cabinet. Seikai-Tensin account for 36.5% (= 1,002/2,746) of the cabinet portfolio in postwar Japan. If we count distinctive individuals rather than posts, this figure increases to 54.4% (= 403/884). Figure 4.1 shows the persistence of Seikai-Tensin throughout the period. At its peak, Yoshida Shigeru, allegedly the most prominent proponent of elite bureaucrats, appointed approximately 67% of the cabinet as former bureaucrats (the 49th cabinet's second reshuffle). While Seikai-Tensin ministers have decreased over time, the influx of newbies keeps them afloat, as Figure 4.2 displays. What makes them constantly needed in the cabinet? What makes them stronger candidates than others with different occupational backgrounds?

As for appointment of Japanese cabinet members, there are two requirements: 1) civilians: As the current constitution was established upon the notion of civil control of the military (文民統制), all cabinet members must be civilians (Constitution §66.2). 2) Members of the Diet: As the Japanese Constitution takes a parliamentary system, the prime minister is to be appointed among members of the Diet (Constitution §67.1).[1] The Constitution (§68) speculates that half of the ministers must be chosen from the Diet, but in reality, almost all ministers are chosen from incumbent legislators. In postwar Japan, only 32 out of 2,756 minister offices (about 1.16%)[2] were filled with people who had *not* ever been a congressperson before getting appointed to the cabinet.

Essentially, cabinet members are heads of ministries. There are ongoing discussions on whether ministers with short tenure could be controlled by, and not control, bureaucrats who stay in a specific ministry for a long time; still, ministers represent the ministry and have official authority over all administrative affairs from approval on policy drafts to appointment and dismissal of bureaucrats. *Then can we say that politicians are more powerful*

DOI: 10.4324/9781003319207-4

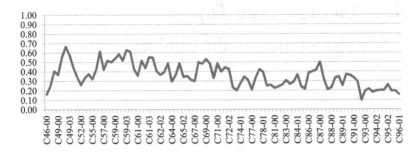

Figure 4.1 Proportion of Seikai-Tensin in the Cabinet

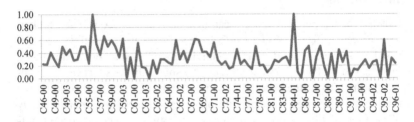

Figure 4.2 Proportion of Seikai-Tensin Among First-Time Ministers

than bureaucrats? This would be the case for many, if not all, countries, but in Japan, answers to the question may be more complex as many cabinet members are ex-bureaucrat legislators, or Seikai-Tensin. About 36.5% of cabinet members (45.3% of prime ministers and 36.0% of ministers) are former bureaucrats. Over one-third of former bureaucrats return to the ministry as its heads. Put differently, there is a confluence of bureaucratic and political careers. This occurs when one becomes a lawmaker after retiring from a ministry; another layer of the blurring of politics and bureaucracy is added when the person is appointed to the cabinet.

This chapter investigates whether Seikai-Tensin politicians are more likely to succeed in the political world than others by testing their likelihood of success in the cabinet. As Table 4.1 exhibits, the number and proportions of Seikai-Tensin politicians have reached a plateau, albeit with some fluctuation from year to year. Ministerial positions are considered the pinnacle of a congressional career, along with the premiership. Cabinet posts are highly sought after because of the greater name recognition and potential electoral benefit they bestow. Elsewhere, achieving cabinet posts has been seen as a career achievement of advancing through electoral tenure and seniority in the party. Many legislators begin their political careers aspiring to be a minister, if not the prime minister, someday;[3] they have "progressive ambition" (Schlesinger 1966) in mind. It is worth noting that one of the most common indicators of ministerial success is how long a minister could survive in the cabinet. In addition, prior background has an effect on minister's capacities to survive (Berlinski et al. 2007).

Table 4.1 Backgrounds of Japanese Ministers: Seikai-Tensin vs. Seshū-Giin

	1953	1963	1972	1983	1993	1998	2001
(a) Seikai-	5	11	7	6	6	5	6
Tensin	(25.0%)	(52.4%)	(33.3%)	(26.1%)	(26.1%)	(20.0%)	(33.3%)
(b) Seshū-	2	3	3	6	6	11	8
Giin	(10.0%)	(14.3%)	(15.7%)	(23.4%)	(24.1%)	(24.4%)	(24.4%)
Tōdai	9	13	9	8	7	7	5
Graduates	(45.0%)	(61.9%)	(42.9%)	(34.8%)	(30.4%)	(28.0%)	(27.8%)
Cabinet Size	20	21	21	23	23	25	18
	(100%)	(100%)	(100%)	(100%)	(100%)	(100%)	(100%)

Source: Colignon and Usui (2003, 150–152)

Note: This table only includes "cabinet members with valid data. The total number of cabinet members was 21 in 1953 and 1963, 24 in 1972, 23 in 1983, 24 in 1993, 25 in 1998, and 18 in 2001. Numbers in parentheses are percentages. Our numbers are smaller because data were missing for some cabinet members" (Colignon and Usui 2003, 152).

Most ministers are members of the Diet; at a lower rate, however, there are a few non-legislator ministers, 24 to be exact, who were appointed between 1947 and 2014. Among the 24, 13 are ex-bureaucrats, 5 are from economic circles, 4 are from educational professions, and 2 are from law. Some of them occupied more than one ministerial post. If we count posts taken by those 24, 20 posts are from ex-bureaucrats, 5 from economics, 6 from education, and 3 from law, which shows even more clearly that former bureaucrats are more likely to be selected without being lawmakers.

Analyzing the Japanese cabinet, there is one caveat. There have been only two breaks in the LDP's one-party rule since 1955. As the prime minister is a leader of the government party (or a coalition of governing parties), and ministers are selected and appointed from the government party, most cabinet members—except for in those two periods—are members of the LDP and its few coalition parties.

The aforementioned caveat can have controlling effects. First, the exceptional periods when the LDP was out of the government (i.e., 1993–1994, 2009–2012) will be tested against the "1955 system" cabinet filled by the LDP and its coalitions. Second, the analyses will partly control for party effects because most of them will be chosen from the LDP, with a very few exceptions, including non-politician ministers, DPJ ministers, and so on. Accepting the shared party membership among most ministers, non-political attributes (i.e., bureaucratic and educational background) would be likely to play a key role in examining determinants of cabinet appointment and tenure.

Cabinet Selection and Personal Attributes

Ministerial Appointment

Roughly, there are two types of personal attributes that can affect cabinet selection. One is personal characteristics that primarily belong to each cabinet nominee, such as demographic characteristics, background, and career path, and the other is political affiliations, such as parties or factions, that are shared with fellow members. Not all scholars distinguish between these two. Fenno (1966, 68–87), who does not distinguish, argues that each nominee must demonstrate unique individual characteristics in order to qualify for a cabinet post. Important considerations include the nominee's party identification, personal loyalty to the president, socio-economic attributes, specialized talents for the position, and geographic origin. Distinguishing the aforementioned two kinds of personal attributes, Cronin (1980, 163) cites the nominee's job qualifications and loyalty to the president as the most important criteria. One aspect of "job qualifications" would be experiences in government administration (King et al. 1984). In making their government, prime ministers would choose the person "best suited" for the task of governing as a minister. Ministers are heads of each ministry and collectively are responsible for running the government. For them, prior knowledge on governmental organizations and administrative procedures would be very useful in commanding the bureaucracy.

Yet it would be an incomplete account to omit political aspects in cabinet selection. Since cabinets are composed of Diet members of the government party, there would be intra-party competitions for ministerial posts. Career ambitions have long been seen as a driving force in explaining legislators' behavior (Schlesinger 1966). For congresspeople, cabinet appointments are considered a significant achievement in their political career. Not only for individual politicians but also for factions within the party, it is in their interests to secure ministerial posts. As party leaders, prime ministers have incentives to use ministerial selection as a tool in managing the career ambitions of their caucus. They put efforts in distributing offices in consideration of desires and demands of individuals and sub-groups within the party. Accordingly, parties develop a regularized system of promotion to manage internal dissent and intra-party politics (Kato 1998; Kam 2006; Nemoto et al. 2008; Nyblade 2013).

In Japan, intra-party competitions have been extended to inter-party levels after the collapse of the LDP's one-party rule in 1993. In 1993, when the LDP lost its majority in the House, anti-LDP/anti-communism parties (非自民・非共産連立政権) formed a coalition government for 11 months; in 1994, the LDP was able to return after two cabinet formations. As Figure 4.3 displays, the composition of cabinets reflects this change; the 79th cabinet (PM Hosokawa Morihiro; August 9, 1993–April 28, 1994) had ministers from eight parties, and the 80th cabinet (PM Hata Tsutomu; April 28, 1994–June 30, 1994) from seven parties. Since then, coalition governments are not rare in Japanese politics. Table 4.2 shows that there is a statistically significant difference between before and after 1993 in light of the number of parties included in the cabinet. Post-1993 cabinets have about 2.6 parties, while pre-1993 ones have 1.2. This implies that prime ministers came to give more consideration to keeping a balance among coalition parties in selecting ministers and that party labels and inter-party competition would now be more critical in cabinet formation compared to when the LDP had sole control over the cabinet. This has generated incentives for party members to unite

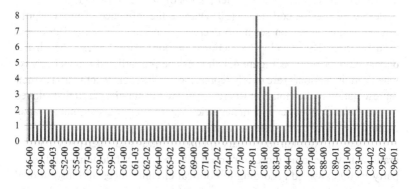

Figure 4.3 Number of Parties Included in the Cabinet

Table 4.2 Party Representation in the Cabinet Pre- and Post-1993

Two-sample t-test with unequal variances: $Pr(|T| > |t|) = 0.0000$, $t = -5.9268$.

Group	Observations	Mean	95% Confidence Interval	
(A) Pre-1993	58	1.19	1.064502	1.314808
(B) Post-1993	36	2.61	2.141039	3.081183
(A) + (B) Combined	94	1.734043	1.496252	1.971833
(A) – (B) Difference		-1.421456	-1.906126	-.9367859

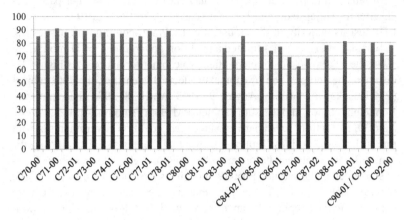

Figure 4.4 Faction Proportionality Index for Cabinet Appointment

under the party platform, while they have to compete with members of the same party as well as those in other parties of their coalition group.

Pekkanen and his colleagues (2014) argue the influence of internal politics on cabinet selection seems to decrease, especially after the 1994 electoral reform. They develop "a factional proportionality index", which has decreased over time, as Figure 4.4 shows. The proportional scores decrease when certain faction(s) are overly represented in the cabinet compared to their representation in the House of Representatives. Put simply, the LDP deployed faction-balancing tactics in a rather strict way to hang together, but as Japan entered the plural party system, balancing *within* the party weakened.

In short, in addition to primary qualities, intra- and inter-party considerations have become more important than before. While intra- and inter-party factors swayed according to political circumstances and institutional changes, the need for administrative expertise would remain steady. Experiences in the bureaucracy are helpful to gain necessary skills and knowledge for ministership. Along with the augmented importance of party labels and balancing within coalitions, former bureaucrats would serve as a constant pool for cabinet members Figure 4.5 succinctly summarizes the previous discussion.

Ministerial Tenure

In analyzing ministerial tenure, there are three kinds of variables to consider: cabinet tenure, portfolio tenure, and personal tenure. Cabinet tenure is the duration between formation and dissolution of cabinets; most ministers

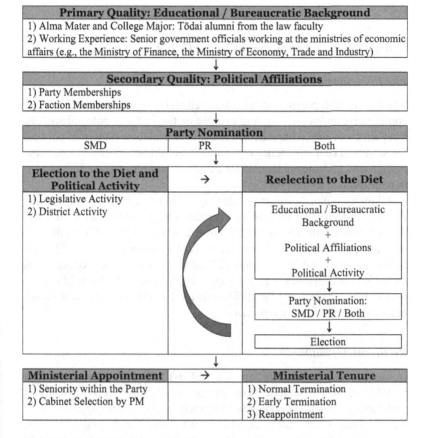

Primary Quality: Educational / Bureaucratic Background
1) Alma Mater and College Major: Tōdai alumni from the law faculty
2) Working Experience: Senior government officials working at the ministries of economic affairs (e.g., the Ministry of Finance, the Ministry of Economy, Trade and Industry)

↓

Secondary Quality: Political Affiliations
1) Party Memberships
2) Faction Memberships

↓

Party Nomination		
SMD	PR	Both

↓

Election to the Diet and Political Activity	→	Reelection to the Diet
1) Legislative Activity 2) District Activity		Educational / Bureaucratic Background + Political Affiliations + Political Activity
		↓
		Party Nomination: SMD / PR / Both
		↓
		Election

↓

Ministerial Appointment	→	Ministerial Tenure
1) Seniority within the Party 2) Cabinet Selection by PM		1) Normal Termination 2) Early Termination 3) Reappointment

Figure 4.5 Seikai-Tensin's Cabinet Appointment Process

are appointed and resign with the whole cabinet; 80% of ministers begin and end their tenure with the cabinet.[4] Portfolio tenure is the average tenure for each ministerial post; it ranges from 94 to 440 days, so it varies across ministries. Personal tenure can be counted for each minister at each cabinet. For various reasons, ministers can be appointed, resign, or be dismissed halfway through cabinet tenure. For appointment, there would be roughly four causes: 1) minister candidates' competence, 2) PM's background and preferences, 3) political circumstances that would affect cabinet reshuffles, and/or 4) creation and abolition of new ministries or cabinet posts. For early termination, there would be two kinds of causes: 1) personal issues such as physical conditions and criminal charges and 2) relational issues such as conflicts within the party and scandalous incidents that create a stir in society.

Seikai-Tensin's Appointment to the Cabinet

The First Appointment

Considering the previous discussion, Seikai-Tensin are assumed to have "progressive ambition", aspiring to move up the ladder of political success. They first move from bureaucracy to the Diet, and the next step of political career would be a ministerial appointment. Would Seikai-Tensin's personal background give them a toehold for fulfilling their progressive ambition, as in their election to the Diet?

All these results, however, would only apply to the LDP regime. In other words, non-LDP governments have certain strategies in recruiting ministers that are different than those of LDP governments. In LDP cabinets, 38.76% of ministers (out of 2,352) are Seikai-Tensin, whereas only 21.53% are Seikai-Tensin (out of 404) in non-LDP cabinets. As for Tōdai background, there also is a difference in proportions, albeit smaller; 38.52% in LDP cabinets and 29.21% in non-LDP cabinets. In a word, elite credentials are much more favored by LDP governments.

Recurrent Appointments

In the previous section, we saw that Seikai-Tensin legislators tend to get their first cabinet appointments earlier than non–Seikai-Tensin legislators in both Houses. Would they continue to be successful in cabinet appointments? Table 4.3 may offer a rather straightforward answer. Employing *t*-tests, one can compare the mean numbers of total cabinet appointments in terms of four individual attributes. Among the cabinet members, those with a bureaucratic background are appointed 2.44 more times, on average, to the cabinet. The "Seikai-Tensin effect" once again appears to be the strongest among others. In non-LDP cabinets, however, Seikai-Tensin and non–Seikai-Tensin ministers hold about the same number of ministerial positions throughout their political careers. Surprisingly, LDP membership does not generate a meaningful difference in the number of cabinet appointments, while Tōdai alumni and male ministers are more frequently appointed to the cabinet.

In the Lower House, a sudden increase occurs on Seikai-Tensin's side between legislative sessions 23 (1947–1949) and 24 (1949–1952). This coincides with the fact that representatives were popular candidates for ministers right after the war when Japan was short of high-quality personnel due to the purge of politicians and soldiers. Former bureaucrats were a reliable source of ministers who could command the bureaucracy,

Table 4.3 Personal Background and Differences in the Number of Cabinet
Appointments (Comparison Among Ministers)

Background	Group	Difference (p-value)		
		All (1947–2014)	LDP Governments	Non-LDP Governments
Bureaucratic	(Seikai-Tensin)	2.44***	2.58***	0.0024
Background	(Non–Seikai-Tensin)	(0.0000)	(0.0000)	(0.9952)
Party	(LDP)	0.64	0.33	0.0051
Affiliation	(Non-LDP)	(0.0053)	(0.2719)	(0.9922)
Educational	(Tōdai)	1.28***	1.40***	0.1432
Background	(Non-Tōdai)	(0.0000)	(0.0000)	(0.6878)
Sex	(Male)	1.62	1.48*	1.74*
	(Female)	(0.0048)	(0.0257)	(0.0363)

Note: p-values are shown in parentheses: *$p < 0.05$, ***$p < 0.001$.

and those in the Lower House were especially recruited. As time has
gone by, the difference between Seikai-Tensin and non–Seikai-Tensin
has decreased, but the former's failure rates are still higher than the
latter's.

Furthermore, right before the second Abe cabinet (the 96th cabinet;
2012–2014), the DPJ ruled Japan from 2009 to 2012. Carrying the banner
of being "politics-oriented" (「政治主導」), the DPJ desired to exclude
bureaucrats from the critical policy-making process. Although it was not
the first time that non–Seikai-Tensin councillors took more ministerial positions than Seikai-Tensin, two factors accelerated non–Seikai-Tensin's failure rates: 1) PM Abe's personal avoidance of Seikai-Tensin and 2) the DPJ's
preferences toward politics, not bureaucracy.

Last, in the Upper House, the sudden increase of non–Seikai-Tensin
after legislative session 23 (2013–2016) indicates that their resignation rates increased recently. In contrast, Seikai-Tensin councillors' exit
rates have gradually developed until the last session. The following
two factors conjointly brought about this change. First, during Upper
House session 23, Abe was in charge for the second time in the 96th
cabinet of Japan (2012–2014). A longtime friend of PM Abe in the Diet
commented:

> Shin-chan [a nickname for Abe Shinzō] hates Tōdai graduates and
> elite bureaucrats. Even among legislators, he doesn't even get along
> with those who graduated from Tōdai. Since his grandfather and father
> were both elites, he may have low self-esteem for he doesn't have
> superior educational background like his family and this may have
> affected his avoidance toward Tōdai graduates and elite bureaucrats.

（「晋ちゃんは東大出身者とエリート官僚が嫌い。議員でも
東大出身者とは肌が合わないのか敬遠する傾向がある。エリー
トだった祖父や父に対する学歴コンプレックスの裏返しではな
いか」とは安倍と付き合いの長い議員の見方だ。」.[5]

Seikai-Tensin's Ministerial Tenure

Would this be a cautionary tale for PMs in forming cabinets? Are Seikai-
Tensin ministers more susceptible to early resignation than non–Seikai-
Tensin? Let's look a bit more deeply into Japanese postwar cabinets.
First of all, we need to make a distinction between "cases" and "individuals." An individual can hold multiple ministerial positions during his or
her political career. On average, Japanese ministers have been appointed
for 3.07 (= 2,756/899) posts. If we collapse the all ministership cases
to unique individuals, Seikai-Tensin ministers, on average, have held
3.51 (= 999/285) ministerial positions, while non–Seikai-Tensin have
2.91 (= 1,757/604). Table 4.4 makes a comparison among individual
ministers (not ministerial posts) by their bureaucratic background; there
is actually no difference between Seikai-Tensin and non–Seikai-Tensin
in terms of their chance of ever having early resignation. Bureaucratic
background is not a deciding factor of duration of ministerial career, as
the Seikai-Tensin effect does not appear significantly in Table 4.4.

Second, however, scrutiny of the reasons for early resignation puts a
new complexion on the previous findings. Table 4.5 lists ministers who

Table 4.4 Proportion of Early Resignation: Seikai-Tensin vs. Non–Seikai-Tensin
(Comparison Among "Unique Individual" Ministers)

Group	N	Mean	95% Confidence Interval	
			Lower	*Upper*
(A) Non–Seikai-Tensin	481	20.37	16.76	23.99
(B) Seikai-Tensin	403	20.35	16.40	24.29
(A) + (B) Combined	884	20.36	17.70	23.02
(A) – (B) Difference		0.02	−5.32	5.37
Ho: diff = 0	$t = 0.0099$		Degrees of freedom = 882	
Ha: diff < 0	Ha: diff != 0		Ha: diff > 0	
$Pr(T < t) = 0.5039$	$Pr(|T| > |t|) = 0.9921$		$Pr(T > t) = 0.4961$	

Table 4.5 Reasons for Early Resignation: Seikai-Tensin vs. Non–Seikai-Tensin

Reason	Seikai-Tensin	Non–Seikai-Tensin	Sum
Personal Liabilities[7]	2.98% (= 12/403)[8]	7.28% (= 35/481)	47
Moral Responsibilities[9]	5	10	15
Political Situation[10]	7	12	19
Position Change[11]	3	7	10
Death	3	2	5
Illness	4	9	13
Other Personal Reason[12]	0	1	1
Sum	8.44% (= 34/403)	15.80% (= 76/481)	110

resigned during their term in office. Seikai-Tensin (2.98%) are less involved with personal liabilities, where a minister him/herself is involved in a disgraceful or unlawful act, compared to non–Seikai-Tensin (7.28%). Among them, there are five ministers who were fired by the prime minister (罷免), as opposed to voluntary resignations. All of them are classified into non–Seikai-Tensin.[6]

While the results suggest a Tōdai background would not aid ministers in holding their ministerial positions for long, LDP ministers tend to remain longer in cabinets compared with their non-LDP counterparts; they have hazard rates 60%–65% higher than those without LDP membership. On the whole, neither personal background (except LDP membership) and electoral experience nor legislative performance affect early resignation from the cabinet. There are largely two explanations for this. First, many ministers resign due to circumstances that are not under their control. As shown in Table 4.5, political situation and moral responsibilities are among the primary reasons for early ministerial termination. In other words, these cases are very much affected by external causes, including macroeconomic factors (Warwick 1994), public opinion (Martin 1999), cabinet approval rates (Masuyama 2002), and power balance in the Diet (Masuyama 2001 for the Lower House; Masuyama 2007 for the Upper House).[13]

Second, early resignation is not common in Japanese cabinets. Most ministers (93%) do not resign until the cabinet dissolves. In most cases, individual ministers' duration would not be much different than cabinet duration (see Huber and Martinez-Gallardo 2004; Nyblade 2011; Masuyama and Nyblade 2015). Cabinet duration would influence Seikai-Tensin and non–Seikai-Tensin alike. Would this imply that Seikai-Tensin's political fortune has ceased to exist?

Table 4.6 Personal Background and Differences in the Total Number of Days in Cabinet (Comparison Among Ministers)

Background	Group	Difference (p-value)		
		All (1947–2014)	LDP Government	Non-LDP Government
Bureaucratic	(Seikai-Tensin)	494.45***	524.82***	−63.22
Background	(Non–Seikai-Tensin)	(0.0000)	(0.0000)	(0.6296)
Party	(LDP)	305.64***	147.02*	−63.11
Affiliation	(Non-LDP)	(0.0000)	(0.0446)	(0.7124)
Educational	(Tōdai)	273.60***	296.93***	−41.42
Background	(Non-Tōdai)	(0.0000)	(0.0000)	(0.7267)
Sex	(Male)	655.78***	622.02**	690.76*
	(Female)	(0.0000)	(0.0001)	(0.0121)

Note: p-values are shown in parentheses; * $p < 0.05$, ** $p < 0.01$, *** $p < 0.001$.

Table 4.6 makes a comparison between groups divided by individual attributes, in light of the total days for which ministers are appointed to the cabinet. Table 4.6 summarizes the results of 12 t-tests. Individual attributes have a very significant influence on one's overall ministerial career. The total number of days for which Seikai-Tensin ministers were appointed significantly surpasses that of non–Seikai-Tensin; bureaucratic background makes a difference of 494 days in cabinet over the course of one's political life. LDP membership and Tōdai background are also useful for ministerial candidates, with an advantage of a bit less than a year. Overall, these three attributes appear to be effective in the LDP government only, but given the LDP's long-lasting rule in postwar Japan, the influence of personal attributes seems to preponderate.

Conclusion

The analysis shows that initial appointment to the cabinet and any subsequent appointments are significantly influenced by whether one has a bureaucratic background. Seikai-Tensin ministers do not remain longer in a given cabinet, but in the long run, they get more posts and have more days in cabinet office. Besides those appointed among members of the Diet, over half are ex-bureaucrats (13 out of 24, 54.17%) among cabinet members who were appointed without being a lawmaker (民間人閣僚), as Table 4.7 shows. Some ministers are appointed for multiple cabinets or multiple positions in a cabinet. Of the ministerial positions taken by

Table 4.7 Non-Legislator Ministers, 1947–2014

Primary Occupation Prior to Cabinet Appointment		Non-Legislator Until *Cabinet* Appointment*		Non-Legislator Even After Cabinet Appointment	
		Case	Person	Case	Person
Seikai-Tensin	Bureaucrat	20	13	20	13
		(58.82%)	(54.17%)	(74.07%)	(68.42%)
Non–Seikai-Tensin	Business	5	5	2	2
		(14.71%)	(20.83%)	(7.41%)	(10.53%)
	Education	6	4	4	3
		(17.65%)	(16.67%)	(1.48%)	(15.79%)
	Law	3	2	1	1
		(8.82%)	(8.33%)	(3.70%)	(5.26%)
Sum		34	24	27	19
		(100.00%)	(100.00%)	(100.00%)	(100.00%)

*Including those elected to the Diet *during* their ministerial tenure.

non-lawmakers, 58.82% are Seikai-Tensin (20 out of 34). This pattern has not faded; among the 14 posts opened up for non-legislators later than 2000, 10 went to ex-bureaucrats.

Also, once a former bureaucrat enters the cabinet, s/he tends to enjoy a longer ministerial tenure, albeit not successive, than those without a bureaucratic background. This is aided by multiple factors; bureaucratic background is a critical factor to be a legislator, which is a necessary (but not sufficient) condition to be a cabinet member; previous records show that those with a bureaucratic background are less likely to be replaced due to various personal liabilities, including criminal convictions and political scandals; Seikai-Tensin's bureaucratic expertise may actually be helpful in serving as a minister who commands a ministry.

Notes

1 The prime minister can either be a councillor or a representative; but since 1947, every prime minister has been a representative.
2 Quite a few ministers were appointed to multiple cabinets and/or were appointed to multiple ministers within a cabinet. If we count the number of distinctive people, instead of that of minister offices, 24 out of 887 postwar ministers (about 2.7%) were not lawmakers at the time of cabinet appointment.
3 By law, the prime minister can appoint 14 civilians (or more, up to 17 on special occasions) as his ministers (Cabinet Law §2.2), but in most cases, the entire cabinet consists of legislators.

4 This includes all ministers but prime ministers. Those who have ever been prime ministers, however, are also included when they are appointed as ministers. Most of them receive a cabinet appointment prior to their premiership.

5 *Weekly Post*, May 29, 2015 (http://news.livedoor.com/article/detail/10131635/; last accessed September 20, 2017).

6 平野力三 (Agriculture & Forestry, November 4, 1947), 広川弘禅 (Agriculture & Forestry, March 3, 1953), 藤尾正行 (Education, September 9, 1986), 島村宜伸 (Agriculture & Forestry, August 8, 2005), 福島瑞穂 (Consumer & Food Safety May 28, 2010).

7 Involvements in bribery scandals, slips of the tongue, and so on (不祥事・疑獄・舌禍).

8 There have been 884 individuals in Japanese cabinets between 1947 and 2014; 403 were Seikai-Tensin and 481 were non–Seikai-Tensin.

9 Not personally liable but resigned due to an unexpected circumstances such as national disasters and tragedies for which one should be held accountable as a minister (引責・罷免・更迭).

10 Neither personally liable nor morally responsible but resigned due to political situations such as the purge by GHQ in the 1940s–50s; political conflicts among factions within parties, mostly in the 1960s; or the need for political reform in the 1990s (閣内対立・政局・公職追放).

11 Moving to another post in the cabinet/Diet, resigning to run for another political office, and so on (衆議院議長に転出・党役員に転出・知事選出馬・総裁戦出馬).

12 Bankruptcy of a privately owned firm (オーナー企業の倒産).

13 The articles by Masuyama (2001, 2002, 2007) investigate the PM's duration only.

Works Cited

Berlinski, Samuel, Torun Dewan, and Keith Dowding (2007). "The Length of Ministerial Tenure in the United Kingdom, 1945–97," *British Journal of Political Science*, 37(2): 245–262.

Cronin, Thomas. (1980). *The State of the Presidency* (2nd ed.). (Boston: Little, Brown and Company).

Fenno, Richard. (1966). *The President's Cabinet*. (Cambridge: Harvard University Press).

Huber, John D., and Cecilia Martinez-Gallardo. (2004). "Cabinet Instability and the Accumulation of Experience in the Cabinet: The French Fourth and Fifth Republics in Comparative Perspective," *British Journal of Political Science*, 34(1): 27–48.

Kam, Christopher, and Indriði Indriðason (2005). "The Timing of Cabinet Reshuffles in Five Westminster Parliamentary Systems," *Legislative Studies Quarterly*, 30(3): 327–364.

Kato, Junko. (1998). "When the Party Breaks Up: Exit and Voice among Japanese Legislators," *American Political Science Review*, 92(4): 857–870.

King, James D., James W. Riddlesperger Jr., and James W. Riddlesperger. (1984). "Presidential Cabinet Appointments: The Partisan Factor," *Presidential Studies Quarterly*, 14(2): 231–237.

Martin, L. W. (2000). Coalition Politics and Parliamentary Government: Essays on Government Formation, Government Survival, and the Legislative Agenda. Ph.D. Dissertation. (Rochester, NY: The University of Rochester).

Masuyama, Mikitaka 増山幹高 (2001). *Agenda Power in the Japanese Diet*. Ph.D. Dissertation. (Ann Arbor, MI: The University of Michigan).

—— (2002). "Government Stability and Economic Changes: Time-Variant Factors in Survival Analysis 「政権安定性と経済変動：生存分析における時間変量的要因」," *Annuals of Japanese Political Science Association* 『年報政治学』, pp. 231–245. Tokyo: Japanese Political Science Association日本政治学会 (Written in Japanese).

—— (2007). "The Survival of Prime Ministers and the House of Councillors," *Social Science Japan Journal*, 10(1): 1–13.

Masuyama, Mikitaka, and Benjamin Nyblade. (2015). "Japan: Ministerial Selection and De-Selection," in *The Selection of Ministers around the World*, pp. 61–83. Keith Dowding and Patrick Dumont (eds.). (New York: Rutledge).

Nemoto, Kuniaki, Ellis Krauss, and Robert Pekkanen (2008). "Policy Dissension and Party Discipline: The July 2005 Vote on Postal Privatization in Japan," *British Journal of Political Science*, 38(3): 499–525.

Nyblade, Benjamin (2011). "The Strengthening of Prime Ministerial Powers and Short Durability 「首相の権力強化と短命政権」," In *Political Parties in Disarray: The Causes and Consequences of the LDP's Fall from Power* 『政党政治の混迷と政権交代』, pp. 245–262. Hiwatari Nobuhiro and J. Saito (eds.). 樋渡展洋・斉藤淳編. (Tokyo: 東京大学出版会 University of Tokyo Press). (Written in Japanese, Translated from English by Matsuda Natsu松田なつ).

—— (2013). "Keeping It Together: Party Unit and the 2012 Election," In *Japan Decides 2012: The Japanese General Election*, pp. 20–33. Robert J. Pekkanen, Steven R. Reed, and Ethan Scheiner (eds.). (London: Palgrave Macmillan).

Schlesinger, Joseph A. (1966). *Ambition and Politics; Political Careers in the United States*. (Chicago, IL: Rand McNally).

Warwick, Paul. (1994). *Government Survival in Parliamentary Democracies*. (Cambridge: Cambridge University Press).

5 Japanese Governance with Intertwined Politics and Administration

Introduction

Throughout this book, the nature of Japanese governance is revealed through Seikai-Tensin's political success in postwar Japan. Japanese governance consists of a fine balance between politics and administration. Both politicians and bureaucrats actively participate in the policy-making process, with different tools and capacities. This complementarity of politics and administration facilitates Seikai-Tensin's transformation and political success. As for individual Seikai-Tensin politicians, it makes it easier to switch to a political career; they can continue to be engaged in policy making with their expertise and skills, which is beneficial both for their career development and the public good. From an institutional perspective, also, Seikai-Tensin's transformation is an efficient way to ensure professionalism in lawmaking; the LDP especially prefers ex-bureaucrats in nominating its candidates. Voters also perceive Seikai-Tensin as being qualified as lawmakers; elite career bureaucrats, who likely graduated from Tōdai and are affiliated with the LDP, fit a general image of statesmen. As such, Seikai-Tensin's perennial political success is well received in Japanese society. All in all, Seikai-Tensin's existence embodies the nature of Japanese policy making, in which politics and administration intersect. This book will ultimately address the nature of Japanese governance, where the key to "the Japanese Miracle" in the past, and the future of Japanese politics, lies.

Bureaucratic culture is deeply embedded in Japanese history and has been institutionalized over time. Japanese bureaucrats have played a significant role in governance and been highly respected in society. Under these conditions, a prestigious bureaucratic career would be the best choice for public service–minded individuals who behave rationally, as it helps them contribute to society while achieving personal career goals (intrinsic motivations). While working as bureaucrats, their preferences for serving the nation and being engaged in policy making are not weakened. However, they realize

DOI: 10.4324/9781003319207-5

there is not much that they can achieve within bureaucracy, and/or politics doesn't do the work despite the vested power (extrinsic factors). All things considered (i.e., bureaucratic culture, individuals' rationality and public service mindset, the nature of governance that gives bureaucrats both policy expertise and frustration), a considerable number of bureaucrats conclude that they would rather become politicians to work in policy making with the strengthened authority bestowed on members of the Diet.

To transform themselves from bureaucrats to politicians, they first need to get elected. When running in congressional elections, they would get more individual vote shares because of their educational and bureaucratic backgrounds, which serve as useful credentials to voters. They also get elected more times on average. Their electoral advantage appears strong even in elections where non-LDP parties take the government.

Furthermore, in the Diet, Seikai-Tensin do not form a distinctive network cluster in terms of their affiliations. Diet members are connected mainly via party memberships. For most of the postwar period, Seikai-Tensin have been located between major political parties. They are not necessarily at the center of major political parties, but they can bridge politicians in other parties at their intermediate locations. Simply put, Seikai-Tensin would have more potential network resources to interact with other lawmakers, inside and outside of the party with which they are affiliated.

Seikai-Tensin's political success continues to cabinet appointments. Seikai-Tensin are more likely to be appointed to a cabinet than those without bureaucratic backgrounds. In terms of a given cabinet, however, Seikai-Tensin's duration is not longer than non–Seikai-Tensin's. In contrast, when we look at a longer period of time, such as the entire political career of a politician, Seikai-Tensin are more likely to be appointed as ministers and remain in office for a longer period of time.

Emergence and Institutionalization of Seikai-Tensin: Seikai-Tensin as Institutions

Throughout previous chapters, we've seen that Seikai-Tensin are naturally accepted in Japanese culture, society, and politics. Thanks to the blurring of politics and bureaucracy, politicians and bureaucrats are perceived as policy makers who work for the country, in spite of many differences between the two. In effect, they work in tandem with each other in the Policy Affairs Research Council (PARC: quasi-governmental apparatus established in the government party) to discuss and draft legislative bills. In a broad sense, there is no essential difference between what bureaucrats and politicians do, as they both are dedicated to state affairs. In that regard, Seikai-Tensin's transformation (i.e., from bureaucrats to politicians) is understood as another way of pursuing state affairs rather than changing career fields to an utterly different one. It may also be viewed as another cross-over of politics and bureaucracy. In all, we can assume that, going back and forth between bureaucracy and politics, Seikai-Tensin play a key role in policy making and in interactions between the government and the government party.

There are pushing and pulling forces that promote Seikai-Tensin's movements between the government and politics. To begin with the pushing forces, the personnel system of the Japanese bureaucracy does not hold up career bureaucrats for their lifetimes. Japanese elite bureaucrats, particularly in the economic ministries, tend to leave their ministries at a relatively young age, in their early 50s. This is quite unusual compared to other countries where there are also strong bureaucracies, in France and elsewhere in Europe, for example.[1] A key factor that helps to explain the phenomenon of early retirement was the unwritten rule within the bureaucracy decreeing that all members of the same entering class in a given ministry should resign as soon as one of them attains the position of administrative vice minister (事務次官), the top of a bureaucratic career. As there is only one vice minister appointed, those who do not see themselves as viable for this position tend to retire early. This practice has served a dual function of sparing the vice minister the embarrassment of having to issue orders to members of his peer group and of clearing the way for advancement of younger officials to senior posts. "The former is an important consideration in Japanese culture, where a strong sense of hierarchy is counterbalanced by an equally strong sense of equality among the cohort" (Koh 1989, 30). Having passed the higher civil-service examination and entered the ministry in the same year, the cohort typically forged extremely close personal ties throughout their government careers. Since Japanese bureaucrats enter and stay in the ministry for their whole careers, this identification with an entering cohort becomes the most important attribute during their bureaucratic life, and it follows them even long after they leave government services (Johnson 1982, 58).

Political parties, especially the LDP, exert pulling forces, on the other hand. The proportions of Seikai-Tensin among LDP legislators suggest that ex-bureaucrats are favored by the government party. Bureaucratic expertise and network resources would certainly be regarded as advantageous for electoral candidates. Additionally, there is no legal restriction put upon Seikai-Tensin's post-retirement movements. In Japan, government retirees are not free to be employed at institutions whose tasks are related to what they took in charge in the government. According to the National Public Service Law (国家公務員法), government employees are not allowed to join a private company for two years after their retirement if they had a close connection with the company within the five years prior to retirement. Every public servant must obtain approval from the National Personnel Authority (人事院) if s/he wants to be employed by a private company before the end of the two-year reemployment limitation (Horiuchi and Shimizu 2001). On the contrary, ex-bureaucrats' midlife career changes to politics are not regulated under the current Japanese Law, although the tasks may be more directly related when moving to politics. In all, the Japanese government and parties do not stop their retirees from becoming legislators but may cause them to do so.

Besides bureaucracy and political parties, there is another institution that contributes to the consistent reproduction of Seikai-Tensin. National universities, including the University of Tōkyō (hereafter Tōdai),[2] serve as a primary pool of elite bureaucrats.[3] Particularly, graduates from the Faculty of Law at Tōdai (東大法学部) prevail in the central bureaucracy. Tōdai graduates are the best in the country in terms of their academic skills and fit nicely into elite bureaucratic positions. At its inception, however, there were plural institutional aids to make Tōdai (then Tōkyō Imperial University, 東京帝国大学) and other national universities reservoirs of high-level bureaucrats. For one thing, in the early Meiji years, Tōdai law (法学部) and literature (文学部) students were given "a free ticket" to enter the bureaucracy; they did not need anything but their diplomas.[4] There were civil service examinations for career bureaucrats, beginning from 1887, but "the function of the examinations was simply to fill positions not claimed by Tōdai graduates" (Spaulding 1967, 91). Later, the government abolished the exemption, but the dominance of Tōdai in ministries did not come to an end.[5] Table 5.1 shows that Tōdai graduates prospered even without any *formal* institutional aids. The two top universities, Tōdai and Kyōdai (Kyōto University 京都大学), together account for seven out of every ten bureaucrats between the abolition of the Tōdai exemption.

We could attribute Tōdai graduates' continued predominance entirely to their abilities and efforts, but there were a couple of reasons they were able to do better than other candidates. While Tōdai outcompeted other universities

Table 5.1 Successful Candidates of Higher Civil Service Examinations, 1894–1947

	1894–1917		1918–1931		1932–1947		1894–1947	
	#	%	#	%	#	%	#	%
Tōdai	1,566	76.3	2,033	57.8	2,370	59.3	5.969	62.4
Kyōdai	101	4.9	379	10.8	315	7.9	799	8.4
Others	385	18.8	1,107	31.4	1,309	32.8	2,797	29.2
Sum	2,052	100.0	3,519	100.0	3,994	100.0	9,565	100.0

Source: Hata (1983).

in the civil service examinations, Tōdai professors also outnumbered others among the examiners, as follows: 46.0% for 1894–1905, 66.0% for 1906– 17, 44.6% for 1918–28, and 41.2% for 1929–41 (Spaulding 1967, 249). The variation corresponds to that of successful examinees from Tōdai for the same time spans: 72.5%, 95.9%, 85.7%, and 67.5% (Spaulding 1967, 251). The numbers suggest that the relationship between examiners and examinees may have affected the results of the exam. It's presumable that the Tōdai examinees' previous exposure to lectures and examinations by such a high proportion of the examiners was bound to be beneficial not only in written but also in oral tests of the civil service examinations.

In addition, the subjects of the exam were designed to be favorable to law students. The administrative examinations from 1894 to 1928 had six required subjects: constitutional law, administrative law, criminal law, civil law, international law, and economics. In addition, candidates were required to select one subject from a set of four electives: criminal procedure, civil procedure, commercial law, and finance (Spaulding 1967, 210). From 1929 to 1941, criminal law and international law were dropped from the list of compulsory subjects; instead, they were added to the greatly expanded list of elective subjects. The other subjects that were newly added were political science, political history, Japanese history, economic history, agricultural policy, industrial policy, social policy, ethics, logic, sociology, psychology, philosophy, and Japanese and Chinese literature. Candidates were required to choose three subjects from the list (Spaulding 1967, 213). Despite the changes from the previous years, the subjects are the ones mostly taught in the Faculty of Law.[6] Currently, there are four core subjects for general candidates: 1) political science/international relations, 2) constitutional law/ administrative law, 3) civil law, and 4) economics/public finance. Except for economics and finance, the rest are taught in the Faculty of Law, and thus law students can still have an advantage over others in the civil service examinations. Accordingly, law students are foremost among Tōdai bureaucrats. Hata (1983) found that a total of 5,969 Tōdai men passed the administrative higher examinations between 1894 and 1947 and that 94.7% of them (N = 5,653) were graduates of its law faculty (17). Between 1947 and 2014, the magnitude of dominance decreases, but they still persist.:72.92% (= 571/783) of Tōdai alumni Seikai-Tensin in the Upper House and 83.74% (= 1,246/1,488) in the Lower House majored in law.

The reason for this apparent favoritism toward the Faculty of Law is largely twofold. First, there is a practical reason for testing law subjects in the examinations. Legal knowledge is essential for public officials, especially in Japan, given their overarching role in the legislative process. Second, as a historical reason, the founding fathers' national design continues to exist today. The Meiji leaders sought to emulate the Prussian model, and requiring legal training as the principal qualification for civil-service appointments is a key factor for law's predominance (Koh 1989, 23).

In summary, three institutions that have contributed to the emergence and evolution of Seikai-Tensin phenomenon are examined. *Pushed* by bureaucracy and *pulled* from political parties, Seikai-Tensin transform themselves from bureaucrats to politicians. The education system spearheaded by Tōdai has served as a persistent source for elite bureaucrats and thus eventually for Seikai-Tensin. These three institutions have created and developed a relationship through formal and informal channels. Seikai-Tensin must have been an *unintended* outcome, but it was supported by all three institutions.

Seikai-Tensin's Dual Identity as Individuals: Seikai-Tensin as Politicians, Bureaucrats, or Both

Seikai-Tensin's transformation is pertinent not only to their affiliated organizations but to their identity as ex-bureaucrats and incumbent legislators. In their dual identity, which one would be stronger than the other? As they are incumbent legislators who were formerly bureaucrats, they could be bureaucrats *as much as* they are politicians. On the other hand, it also sounds plausible that their bureaucratic identity would be subsumed under their politician identity, which implies a lower influence of bureaucratic identity. This question is critical, as it would eventually lead to a bigger question as to the general relationship between politicians and bureaucrats and also between the government and political parties.

Some would argue that, for Seikai-Tensin, their bureaucratic background would be strong, at least as strong as their current occupation as politicians. For one thing, bureaucratic background is an important prerequisite for politicians, *when recruited by political parties and/or elected in elections*. It is not clear among bureaucratic qualifications what specifically made them politicians, though. It could be either expertise accumulated while in the government, personal networks from the college and ministry, academic competency proven by their alma maters, having been career bureaucrats, or all of the previously mentioned. In any event, however, being ex-bureaucrats is a plus for those who want to become politicians.

Additionally, according to this view, *during their legislative tenure*, Seikai-Tensin as individual lawmakers would play a key role in the legislative process, due to their distinctive background as ex-bureaucrats. Legislative skills learned through work experience at the government could be useful, while networks built in the government could be a valuable asset. It is likely that Seikai-Tensin would be located between bureaucracy and politics. Currently being a legislator, one can work closely with their former colleagues in the government.

Others would oppose to this view, in that Seikai-Tensin's current occupation is more weighted than the previous one. Once transformed, Seikai-Tensin would act as politicians rather than as ex-bureaucrats. A key contributing factor to this "complete metamorphosis" would be the formidable power held by the LDP in the legislative process, distributive politics, and campaign finance. The government party possesses strong control over legislation, budget, pork, and political money, which are arguably the most important resources to legislators, especially for their reelection. Most legislative bills, including budget and pork, passed in the National Diet are introduced as government bills that have gone through deliberations in PARCs in the LDP. Seikai-Tensin may contribute to the PARC deliberations with their bureaucratic expertise, but their contribution would not be explicitly disclosed in public so that they could get a personal credit for it. Legislative bills are drafted by bureaucrats, co-signed with party members. Thus there is little room for claiming personal credit for their legislative efforts. Instead, they get to invest in the party to get legislative bills passed and acquire necessary resources for their election.

This view values collective membership in a party more than individual skills and efforts in creating one's identity. Rather than being someone possessing specialized expertise, Seikai-Tensin become a part of politics after the transformation. Under these circumstances, non–Seikai-Tensin politicians would also be grouped by their party memberships or other attributes acquired after entering politics such as legislative committee memberships, political faction memberships, and so on. Apart from their pre-political career, legislators would gather around the flag of their party. This does not mean, however, that the individual characteristics of each legislator are all removed. It is only to say that personal attributes become less conspicuous than their party and/or political affiliations.

Conclusion

Many Japanese bureaucrats articulate that their motivation is founded in the congruence of personal and public values (Park 2017). For young, bright minds, a bureaucratic career seems to be the best way to fulfill their ambition to serve the nation while achieving recognition and elite status. As we saw in Chapter 2, this has deep roots in Japanese history and bureaucratic culture tracing back to the premodern period and the founding fathers' institutional design at the outset of modern Japan. The Invisible Hand, aided by various factors, forms a harmony of personal success and public good in the Japanese government. This "blessing" has been said to be *the* principal reason for the Japanese Miracle (see especially Johnson 1982).

However, it comes as a surprise that many of those dedicated bureaucrats dropped out of the government. In interviews, most Seikai-Tensin quit midway either because they couldn't endure the weakness of bureaucracy or because they decided to rectify the faults of politics. In addition, career concerns appear to matter to some extent. How can we interpret the dilemma of Seikai-Tensin's transformation (i.e., exit from the bureaucracy and entering politics)? There are roughly two perspectives, one from public administration and the other from political science.

To begin with, in light of human resources management, we need to evaluate the meaning of Seikai-Tensin's retirement from the government. Seikai-Tensin's transformation occurs within the government and the Diet, both of which are governmental organizations. Seikai-Tensin take part in policy making, either before or after retirement from the government. Thus it may be hard to view Seikai-Tensin's early retirement as brain drain. Seikai-Tensin's bureaucratic background turned out to be useful in achieving political success (see Chapter 3 for election and Chapter 4 for cabinet appointment), but it is not expressed by Seikai-Tensin that government posts were their stepping stones to the Diet and the cabinet. They instead express disappointment in politics and the government, which they explain as the main causes for their transformation. That is, it was not (entirely) a strategic career choice to fulfill progressive ambition; rather, there was a reason inherent in the bureaucracy and/or politics that made them leave. To redress the problem, yet in a different capacity, they chose to be a politician; they say:[7]

(When I was a bureaucrat,) I had many ups and downs, but I was so much attracted to what I was working on. I really wanted to get involved in tasks like legislation and taxation as they were directly relevant with authority and power, as much as I continue to do such things even if I retire from the government. . . . While I was thinking I would be able to work with more strengths if I were a politician, (a political party) contacted me; so I thought "This is my destiny". [（官僚の時）いろいろありましたが、確かに仕事の魅力が大きかったです。法律や税制の仕組み作りなど直接的に権力に携われるということは、官僚を辞めてもやりたいと思うくらいでした。 . . . 政治家になれば、もっと力を入れて働けるんじゃないかと思っていたときに（政党から）声が掛かったんで、これは運命だなと感じました。]

(Seikai-Tensin councillor)

Many young Japanese bureaucrats quit for various reasons. Among them, Seikai-Tensin choose political careers. It may not be a loss for the country, but for the government, the constant outflow of young elite bureaucrats can make it hard to nurture career public officials with bureaucratic expertise, which could ultimately affect the quality of national policy. This "small-N" interview project would not be able to prove *all* motivational factors for *all* Seikai-Tensin politicians. But it is worth noting that Seikai-Tensin's transformation is in large part a result of disincentivized bureaucrats. This represents the current working environment of Kasumigaseki, in which potential Seikai-Tensin reside. This is not an ideal condition for the overall Japanese governance system, although Seikai-Tensin legislators' contributions would make up for the loss in government personnel by demonstrating their skills and expertise learned while working in the government (the topic of work in progress). The incentive structure of the Japanese bureaucracy seems to have much room for improvement. Ideally, the interview data collected from this project could serve as a cornerstone for an administrative reform.

Second, Seikai-Tensin's transformation can also be viewed from a political science perspective, as it addresses a puzzle found in *the relationship between the elite and electoral democracy*. Seikai-Tensin's transformation is democratic in that it occurs through the electoral mechanism rather than through an arbitrary means. It was their decision to retire from the government, but they couldn't be Seikai-Tensin if not selected by people. Public support is essential for Seikai-Tensin's transformation. This differs from other types of elite transformation in Japan, such as Amakudari (天下り), Yokosuberi (横滑り), and Wataridori (渡り鳥), which occur during coordination between ministries and relevant organizations (e.g., private companies, public corporations) (Colignon and Usui 2003).[8] Seikai-Tensin also differ from hereditary politicians (see Table 1.3 for how they substantially differ), as they inherit so-called san-ban (三バン): family wealth (kaban 鞄), reputation (kanban 看板), and political network and social organization (jiban 地盤). These resources are then converted into election to political office. In that sense, the political legitimacy embodied in Seikai-Tensin politicians primarily comes from the procedural legitimacy of the electoral mechanisms. As can be expected, it is not easily come by as Amakudari privilege or san-ban. Seikai-Tensin themselves do not take their political success for granted:

> If you want to be a politician, you should win an election no matter what. As such, it was tough for me (to get elected) because I did not have any knowledge on how elections work. . . . Especially, during the first 3–4 months of campaign, I didn't have a secretary. So I had to do everything all by myself, such as putting posters, drive, schedule management, etc. It was so hard. . . . I thought after the election that everyone supported me who does not have any connection, hereditary background. I am deeply thankful for the support. (政治家になろうっ て思ったらどうしても選挙に通らなければならない。その点で

は選挙というものの知識は０で選挙に臨んだので厳しかったで
す。特に最初の３〜４か月は秘書もいなくて、ポスター貼り、
運転、スケジュール管理など何から何まですべて一人でやらな
ければいけなかったので選挙活動はとても大変でした。．．．選
挙の後いろいろ思うんですが、地縁血縁ではなく公募で選ばれ
た私に対して、皆さんが力を貸してくれることが、どれほどあ
りがたいことだろうか、と感じます。）

(Seikai-Tensin representative)

Bureaucrats' decision to be Seikai-Tensin involves consideration of potential risks. As rational individuals, they would not retire and run for an election if expected costs exceeded expected benefits. It seems rather risky to
give up government posts with guaranteed tenure and to choose a political
office that is up for election frequently. An incumbent Seikai-Tensin representative says his desire for good policy overcomes ambition for reelections, as opposed to Fenno (1978)'s claim regarding US representatives:

In the first place, I would not have entered a risky field like this, if I
just wanted to be a Member of the Diet. Only with one election or two,
it would not be possible to make the country as I want it to be. . . . So
it's not like I want to make an achievement in just one thing, an election to the Diet for example. I want to be a politician to represent this
era by working on current issues or urgent crisis in the present time.
(そもそも、国会議員になることで満足するようであれば、こ
んなにリスクの大きな世界に飛び込むことはしません。１、
２回当選しただけでは、私自身が実現したい国造りなどでき
ません。．．．だから当選とかなにか１つのことだけがやりたい
わけじゃなくて、その時期に起こる様々な出来事や危機にき
ちんと対応して、その時期を代表する政治家のひとりになり
たいと思います。）

(retired bureaucrat defeated in election)

It may be hard to make a generalization about motivational factors that
give rise to Seikai-Tensin's transformation. But we cannot deny that Seikai-
Tensin take a considerable amount of risks when giving up bureaucratic
posts. Most of them do not have a hereditary background that they can rely
on, as Table 1.3 shows. All of the 14 Seikai-Tensin interviewees included
in this study did (or do) not have connections to politics when still working
at the government. Their relationship building started shortly before their
entrance into politics. In terms of *the relationship between the elite and
electoral democracy*, it would be ideal that committed elites take risks for
the public good. This is mirrored in the myth of the Japanese miracle, as the

literature depicts that bureaucrats' common orientation generally refers to their "broad custodial responsibilities" for the nation (Fukui 1987, 369).

To sum up, Seikai-Tensin's transformation from bureaucrats to politicians involves various motivational and preference factors: *aptitudes for public posts, congruence of personal interests and public values, progressive ambition, strategic career choices, a feeling of helplessness toward politics and the government, risk-seeking preferences,* and *devotion to good policy,* to name a few. They choose a bureaucratic career, as it satisfies both their personal interests and (their ambition to contribute to) the public good. They leave the government because of frustrations toward bureaucracy, resolution to reform politics, and career concerns.

This presents a bit of a different picture of Japanese governance than *developmental state theory.* DST argues that the dramatic economic development of some East Asian countries in the late 20th century was fueled by *bureaucratic autonomy.* Chalmers Johnson (1982) coined this term based on his study of Japanese political economy, and it has been applied to other cases such as South Korea, Singapore, Taiwan, and China. DST identifies the state with the bureaucracy; the strong bureaucracy wields power and guides society to develop the state economy of Japan. On the other hand, other political/governmental institutions, including the National Diet, are largely overlooked. The existence of Seikai-Tensin, however, reveals the complementarity of politics and administration. In Japan, bureaucrats draft legislative bills, while politicians set policy priorities that shape the direction of the policy drafts written in the government. Japanese bureaucrats certainly have a critical influence on the policy process in terms of their policy expertise, and politicians need their aid in dealing with policy matters. Bureaucratic autonomy, however, is substantially limited by politicians' political decisions. Politicians' intervention level depends on importance of the policy issues; when considered important, politicians are heavily involved in making policy; otherwise, they delegate a substantial part of policy making to bureaucrats. In sum, bureaucrats and politicians are influenced by each other to varying degrees depending on the circumstances. Bureaucratic authority is constrained by power inherent in the Diet, whereas the Diet's limited policy expertise, lacking in detail, produces room for bureaucratic empowerment. This is, however, not to deny the power of Japanese bureaucrats and their contribution to the miraculous economic development. The bureaucratic power to guide politics and society is a foundation of Seikai-Tensin's transformation and political success. Still, Seikai-Tensin's persistence, that is, the continued flow of ex-bureaucrats to the Diet throughout the postwar period, sheds light upon the nature of Japanese governance, that is, the complementarity of politics and administration. The Japanese policy process can best be explained by the intertwined relationship of politicians and bureaucrats and Seikai-Tensin.

Notes

1 "Retirement: Amakudari ('Descent from Heaven')" (http://afe.easia.columbia. edu/at/jp_bureau/govtjb09.html, last accessed on September 1, 2022).

2 Tōdai (東大) is the abbreviation for the University of Tōkyō (東京大学). For some reason, the Japanese have tended to use Tōdai more often than its official name, and it gradually came to have a particular connotation referring to its fame and societal influence.

3 One may argue that, for the Japanese, educational background should include primary and secondary schools, but this book only considers colleges, as they are directly related to recruitment of elite bureaucrats. The Japanese education system is so systematically organized that elite primary and secondary schools are aligned with prestigious colleges. For instance, many Japanese universities run educational institutions from kindergarten to high school. Once admitted, students usually advance to the next grade and/or the upper school without having to take entrance exams at each level, like they are taking an "escalator" all the way up to college. Considering the difficulty and competitiveness of college entrance exam, many Japanese parents urge their children to get into one of these escalator schools, preferably from kindergarten. Keio University and Chūo University are known to be popular among these escalator schools. As the "escalator school system" (エスカレーター学校: esukarētā-gakkō) displays, the Japanese often say that "one's life is determined at kindergarten". The "escalator" does not stop at college; rather, it takes the people on it up to their first employment after college graduation and beyond—particularly so in the case of Seikai-Tensin politicians.

4 Tōdai graduates were also given the exemption privilege for bar examinations (since 1876) and judicial appointments (1884).

5 "The government's decision in 1893 to abolish the Imperial University exemption stemmed not simply from its desire to accommodate the critics of the privilege but also from the practical need to cope with growing numbers of Tōdai graduates" (Koh 1989, 19; pronunciation mark added by the author).

6 Note that Japanese academic divisions at universities are unique. The size and scope of the Faculty of Law (法学部) are broader than one may think. It may differ by school, but political science, public policy, and other relevant majors are also included.

7 All of the interviews included in this book were conducted based on the questionnaire, which has been approved by the University of Chicago Social and Behavioral Sciences Institutional Review Board (SBS-IRB) for Human Subjects (IRB15–0246).

8 In their transformation, Seikai-Tensin develop a close relationship with political parties from the candidate nomination stage. But it's not arranged by ministries or governmental personnel agency, as other post-bureaucratic destinations are. In most cases, the political party contracts a potential candidate, or an individual applies for an open primary.

Works Cited

Fenno, Richard F. (1978). *Home Style: House Members in Their Districts*. (Boston: Little, Brown).

Hata, Ikuhiko 秦郁彦 (1983). *Study of Bureaucrats: Eternal Power: 1868–1983* 『官僚の研究—不滅のパワー・1868-1983』. (Tokyo: Kodansha 講談社). (Written in Japanese).

Horiuchi, Akiyoshi, and Katsutoshi Shimizu (2001). "Did Amakudari Undermine the Effectiveness of Regulator Monitoring in Japan?," *Journal of Banking & Finance*, 25(3): 573–596.

Johnson, Chalmers A. (1982). *MITI and the Japanese Miracle: The Growth of Industrial Policy: 1925–1975*. (Palo Alto: Stanford University Press).

Koh, B. C. (1989). *Japan's Administrative Elite*. (Berkeley: University of California Press).

Park, Nara (2017). *The Nature of Japanese Governance: Seikai-Tensin (*政界転身*)'s Political Success in Postwar Japan, 1947–2014*. Ph.D. Dissertation. (Chicago, IL: The University of Chicago).

Spaulding, Jr., Robert M. (1967). *Imperial Japan's Higher Civil Service Examinations*. (Princeton: Princeton University Press).

Index

Note: numbers in **bold** indicate a table. Numbers in *italics* indicate a figure.